"I do believe that there is a lot more known about extraterrestrial investigation than is available to the public right now [and] has been for a long time.... It's a long, long story. It goes back to World War II when all of that happened, and is highly classified stuff."

Dr. Edgar Mitchell
Astronaut

PLATES 1 & 2
NAZI FOO FIGHTER?
DONOR & CREATOR
G. W. Dodson

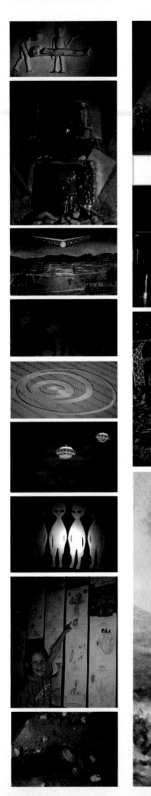

What Do You Think?

PLATE 17
MUSEUM COLLAGE

PLATE 17

Museum Collage

RETROFIT
BAS-RELIEF
ARTIST & DONOR
Bob Turner

ALIEN WATERFALL
DONOR
Ashley Waterfall Co.

HUDSON VALLEY
UFO
ARTIST & DONOR
Joan Laurino

DRAWING OF ET
Artist Unknown

OLIVER'S CASTLE
CROP CIRCLE
PHOTOGRAPHER &
DONOR
Barbara Lamb

GULF BREEZE
SIGHTING
ARTIST & DONOR
Joan Laurino

WE HAVE FIVE OF
THEM
ARTIST & DONOR
Markus Tracy

CHILDREN'S ART
Museum Visitor
Tess Renee Dilmore

CRASHED SAUCER
CREATOR & DONOR
Rodney Hosler

MIDDLE COLUMN
MILITARY RETRIEVAL
ARTIST & DONOR
G. W. Dodson

ROSWELL INCIDENT
MURAL
ARTIST & DONOR
Miller Johnson

GOLDEN FLYING
SAUCER
(Above mural)
ARTISTS
At Mesa Middle
School
DONORS
Dusty & Heidi
Huckabee

WM. HERRMANN
ABDUCTION
ARTIST & DONOR
Joan Laurino

RETURN TO
ROSWELL
ARTIST
Howard Rees
DONOR
Bruce Meland

RIGHT COLUMN
OLD BARNS AND
ALIEN OBJECTS
ARTIST & DONOR
Von Tipton

SAUCER DRAWING
Museum Visitor
Robby Dilmore III

FLYING SAUCERS
APPEARED IN THIS
WEAVING
UNPLANNED
WEAVER
Bella Sue Martin

SCORPION OR
FLYING COMET
CROP CIRCLE
PHOTOGRAPHER &
DONOR
Barbara Lamb

PATROLMAN H.
SHIRMER GOING
ABOARD CRAFT
ARTIST & DONOR
Joan Laurino

T-SHIRT HEAVEN
INSIDE MUSEUM

SAUCER OUTSIDE
MUSEUM
ARTIST & DONOR
Chuck
Beauchemin

MUSEUM NEON
SIGN

IUFOMRC

INTERNATIONAL UFO MUSEUM
AND
RESEARCH CENTER (IUFOMRC)
ROSWELL, NEW MEXICO

ROSWELL
HAVE YOU WONDERED?

UNDERSTANDING THE EVIDENCE OF UFOS
AT THE INTERNATIONAL UFO MUSEUM
AND RESEARCH CENTER

BY
C.P. LEACOCK

Letter from Colonel Philip J. Corso, U.S. Army, (Ret.)
Author of THE DAY AFTER ROSWELL

NOVEL WRITING PUBLISHERS
Ann Arbor, Michigan

Novel Writing Publishers
© 1998 by C.P. Leacock
All rights reserved. First edition 1998
Protected under the Berne Convention
Printed in the United States of America

05 04 03 02 01 00 99 98   8 7 6 5 4 3 2 1

Photo Credits: C.P. Leacock and G.M. Leacock
Research Assistant: Marjorie B. Giebitz
Cover Artists: Von Tipton and Barb Gunia
Cover Layout: Barb Gunia and C.P. Leacock

Publisher's-Cataloging in Publication
Leacock, C.P., 1951-
Roswell: have you wondered? Understanding the evidence of
UFOs at the International UFO Museum and Research
Center/C.P. Leacock
    p.   cm.

Includes bibliographic references and index.
LCCN 98-85669
ISBN 0-9661329-1-2
ISBN 0-9661329-0-4 (pbk.)

1. Unidentified flying objects—Sightings and encounters—New
Mexico—Roswell. 2. Unidentified flying objects—Social aspects
3. Unidentified flying objects-personal narratives 4. Human-
alien encounters 5. Art-Unidentified Flying Objects
6. International UFO Museum and Research Center—
Exhibitions I. Leacock, C.P. 1951-   II. Title
TL789.3.L   1998
001.942-dc21   98-85669
                                               CIP
The paper used in this publication meets the minimum require-
ments of the American National Standard for Information
Sciences—Permanence of Paper for Printed Library Materials,
ANSI Z39.48-1984.

Permissions To Print

Many thanks to those people and companies that so generously granted permission to reprint quotes or print photographs of their art.

"Roswell 1947" and "Old Barns & Alien Objects" used by permission of Tipton's Fantasy Art, Von Tipton, 8051 Joseph St., Sneads, FL 32460. 850-593-0086. "We Have Five of Them" used by permission of Markus W. Tracy, 764 E. Twain Ave. #13G, Las Vegas, NV 89109. "The Survivor" used by permission of Voyager Promotions. Michael Mackey, P.O. Box 54941, Lexington, KY 40555-4941. Flying Saucer Weaving used by permission of Bella Sue Martin, Smithsonian Invitational Artist, P.O. Box 1238, Ranchos De Taos, NM 87557. "Military Retrieval at the Roswell Crash" used by permission of Vincent Dumond, UFO Features, 27 Rue des Rancy, 69003 Lyon, FRANCE. Fax 011-33-04-7895-3089.

Disclaimers

To the Brave

Contents

Foreword by Walter Haut

Co-Founder of the International UFO Museum
and Research Center
&
Witness to Events
from the Roswell Incident

Walter Haut (left) with Museum co-
founder Glenn Dennis

Once upon a time (some days it feels like yesterday and
other days it seems like an eternity) it was my fortune to
put out a press release that shook the world. As the
Public Relations Officer for Roswell Army Air Field and
the 509th Bombardment Group, I wrote a story for the
news media that created interest and skepticism.

It is not that this was a common experience or
something put together by fiction writers. It was factual.
On July 8, 1947 upon the authority of Colonel William H.
Blanchard, base commander, I put out a story which in
essence stated that the base had come into possession of
a flying saucer. This object was recovered from a ranch
north of Roswell, having been located by a ranch hand
who brought pieces of it to the sheriff's office and RAAF.

When the news of this hit the wire services,
reporters immediately started calling the base and a large
majority of the calls came to the Public Relations Office.

We made every effort to assist the media, but because we hadn't seen the material, about all we could tell them was that the material was found on a ranch north of Roswell, pieces were brought to the base, and then taken to higher headquarters at Fort Worth, Texas.

There has to be a humorous side to all stories and this one was no exception. According to the reports, the disc, after being examined at the base, was flown to higher headquarters. The wording "flown to higher headquarters" prompted the question that was asked by most callers. "How did Major Marcel know how to fly this object?" *He did not!* The material was put on board an aircraft which carried the material to its destination.

The following day the whole story took a different turn when General Roger M. Ramey, Commander of the 8th Air Force, cleared up the whole matter. He stated that the debris was simply a harmless, high-altitude weather balloon. When the General states that something is a weather balloon, it is a weather balloon!

For the more than fifty years following the event, I have talked to literally thousands of people who call me, write me, or stop by my home to talk about this incident. Things really got warmed up when Stanton T. Friedman visited me at my home and interviewed me. The information I gave him was included in *The Roswell Incident*, which Charles Berlitz and William Moore wrote. This book was published in 1980 and was the start of a continual flow of journalists contacting me. It seems as if each year more and more writers are using UFOs as their subject.

As time went on and more people began taking an interest in the subject, it became apparent that there should be greater dissemination of information regarding UFOs. In 1990, I was asked to take part in a seminar on UFOs sponsored by the Fund for UFO Research. It was a very enlightening series of meetings wherein many views and opinions were expressed. This gave me more of an incentive to go further with the idea of creating a UFO museum in Roswell. I discussed this idea with Glenn

Dennis (see his story, pages 27 and 28) and he concurred that we should create a museum. After a presentation to a local organization, another individual, Max Littell, was very interested and joined the two of us in establishing a UFO museum. After all of the legal ramifications were taken care of, we found a short-term home on the seventh floor of a bank building, collected donated office furniture, and bought a display of UFO materials. I was the first president, Glenn Dennis, the vice-president and Max Littell, the secretary-treasurer. We offered memberships to the first 100 people with a $100 donation. It was surprising how quickly we had the first 100 members.

Almost immediately we realized that in order to attract visitors to the museum, we had to change our location. We moved to quarters a block away where we stayed until January 1997. Then we moved to the present location, a former movie theater, with space for a much larger display area with more displays, and the operation of an extensive gift shop.

If it were not for the multitude of volunteers who put in many hours of service, this operation could not continue. Even though I feel like I am the original founder of the museum, without the volunteers' assistance, it would not have grown as it has.

The Roswell Incident occurred; fifty plus years have elapsed; and still a multitude of unanswered questions remain. Perhaps in the next millennium the answers will come forth and all the truth will be exposed.

Walt Haut
March 21, 1998
Roswell, New Mexico

Colonel Philip J. Corso, U.S.
Army, (Ret.) photographed in
1959 after receiving the command of 7th Army Inspector
General at the age of 43.

Letter to IUFOMRC Visitors
Colonel Philip J. Corso, U.S. Army, (Ret.)

Author of THE DAY AFTER ROSWELL

&

Witness to the Debris and Bodies
from the Roswell
Incident

Dear Visitor,

The Museum highlights the UFO craft and the extraterrestrial biological entity (ebe) that crashed in Roswell in July 1947. Little did any of us realize at the time that the craft and the ebe were one. One couldn't function without the other. Both the craft and the ebe were of the same basic structure and composition. They survived and functioned within the electromagnetic envelope that acted as their environment.

During the Golden Years of Research and Development, 1959-1963, many technological projects were conceived by the Army from that UFO craft. At that time, the main purpose was national security, to give our army the "competitive edge." Secondly, we wanted to move these great discoveries by "applied engineering" into industry, to benefit the U.S. citizens and the world. The refinement and further development of these marvelous concepts continue to this day and will continue and will affect our future.

I wrote *The Day After Roswell*, detailing this momentous time, mainly for our youth. I have had hundreds of young people come to me and thank me for letting them know the truth. The future is theirs and the heavens are theirs to explore. I promise them many more revelations. A new science will be born to pave their way into space. Many people, like myself, the IUFOMRC members and others, will not allow the truth of UFOs or the future

technology they provide to be taken from our youth (including my grandchildren).

The world has yet to recognize what it owes the International UFO Museum and Research Center. The future has just begun and they are showing the way. I wish to extend my recognition and gratitude to the members of the International UFO Museum and Research Center. These people have had the foresight, knowledge, and courage to move forward with what they know despite any and all opposition. I would like to recognize especially: Glenn Dennis, Walter Haut, Deon Crosby and all the volunteers.

> Sincerely,
> Philip J. Corso
> Col. U.S. Army (Ret.)
> March 5, 1998

Preface

I explored the International UFO Museum and Research Center for the first time the week after the 50th anniversary of the Roswell Incident; then wished I had something to read about the exhibits. I had read many books about UFOs and extraterrestrials over the years, but wanted to revisit my unique experience in the Museum. A book about the Museum wasn't available at that time, so as a writer, I eagerly proposed and accepted the job of producing a book so others could recreate their Museum adventure or plan a visit to Roswell.

As I sifted through all the information supporting the evidence in the Museum, I kept asking myself: How could I convey to you, the reader, the volumes of documentation pointing to extraterrestrial life on earth, both ancient and modern? It grows daily. How could I explain that Pandora may never be able to shut this box again? Many historical mysteries begin to make more sense not less in light of UFOs and extraterrestrials. How could I help you cope with the preponderance of evidence, if it is new to you or has broken through an old belief?

The first third of the Museum concerns the Roswell Incident, as it has come to be known. The rest of the collection covers a broad overview of the UFO and extraterrestrial phenomena: sightings, crop circles, ancient astronauts and abductions. This edition follows the basic Museum outline with some exhibit photographs and documents with additional supporting information. I did not try to rewrite lengthy evidence, but directed you to other references.

I plan to continue to do research and update this information in annual editions. You, the reader, will have access to a consistent overview through time of changes in the Museum, further research and evidence of UFOs and extraterrestrials. Updated editions will be available through the IUFOMRC or Novel Writing Publishers.

C.P. Leacock
May 20, 1998

Introduction

Welcome to the International UFO Museum and Research Center. There are millions of UFO stories on the naked earth...these are a few of them. The evidence is here. Read it all, then decide what you think.

This guide is organized in order of the major exhibits of the Museum. The floor plan and key follow on the next pages (see pages 2 and 3).

The narrative in this guide is not a word-for-word reproduction of the information from each exhibit. The information is paraphrased and added to additional information from research gathered from many sources noted in the text like this: (Author last name, date of copyright) and found in the References. The References are user friendly with short descriptions of each book so that you may follow up with your own research, if you wish. There are many excellent UFO books and articles not listed in References. The references used for this book were intended to be a review of some literature directly related to Museum exhibits but not a complete reference to all UFO writing that may apply.

Many of the individuals you see in the Museum are volunteers dedicated to providing service to our visitors. They would be glad to help you in any way they can during your visit to the Museum. Just don't be surprised by their maturity. Many people are amazed at the average age of the volunteers, many of whom were already in their adult years at the time of the Roswell Incident.

THE
INTERNATIONAL
UFO MUSEUM
COLLECTION

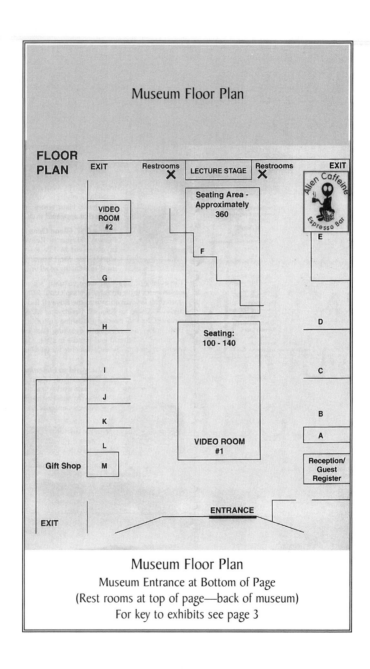

Museum Floor Plan

FLOOR PLAN

EXIT | Restrooms ✕ | LECTURE STAGE | Restrooms ✕ | EXIT

VIDEO ROOM #2

Seating Area - Approximately 360

F

E

G

H

Seating: 100 - 140

D

I

C

J

K

B

L

VIDEO ROOM #1

A

Gift Shop | M

Reception/ Guest Register

ENTRANCE

EXIT

Museum Floor Plan
Museum Entrance at Bottom of Page
(Rest rooms at top of page—back of museum)
For key to exhibits see page 3

MUSEUM EXHIBITS—Key to Page 2

Exhibit A
Alien Examination — See Chapter 1

Exhibit B
Roswell Incident Timeline — See Chapter 2

Exhibit C
Roswell Incident Timeline Part II — See Chapter 2

Exhibit D
Mogul Balloon Display — See Chapter 3
Roswell Case Closed by the Air Force
Anthropomorphic Crash Dummy

Section E
ALIEN CAFFEINE ESPRESSO BAR

Section F
Auditorium Area

Exhibit G
Crop Circles — See Chapter 5
Ancient Civilizations and ETs — See Chapter 6

Exhibit H & I
Poetry, Personal Experiences,
Photographs and Diagrams of UFOs — See Chapter 7

Exhibit J
Our Universe — not included in guidebook

Exhibit K
The 1996 Metal Fragment Incident — Chapter 8

Exhibit L
Humor and UFOs

Section M — Tour Information Office

GREY E.T.
DONOR
G. W. Dodson

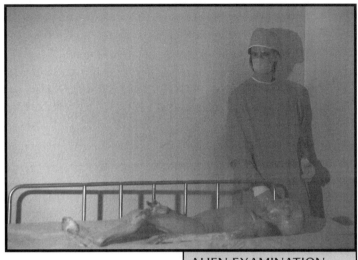

ALIEN EXAMINATION
ALIEN DONOR
Paul Davids
Executive Producer
SHOWTIME ORIGINAL: ROSWELL
CREATOR
Steve Johnson

CHAPTER 1
Exhibit A
Alien Examination

This movie-prop alien is about to undergo an examination. This scene portrays the evidence that examinations were performed on aliens from the Roswell crash in 1947. A nurse (name withheld), a physician (La June Foster, MD), a mortician (Glenn Dennis) and an intelligence officer in the Army (Colonel Philip Corso) have all discussed the examinations and the findings (Dennis 1991; Randle and Schmitt 1994; Corso 1997).

The Paul Davids Exhibit

Alien Examination

Special effects artist, Steve Johnson, the creator of the slimer in *Ghostbusters,* and his crew produced this model of an alien for the *Showtime Original* movie *Roswell.*

Jeremy Kagan, *Roswell* director/producer, filmed the story of the Roswell incident in 1993. The script was written by Arthur Kopit. The stars of the film included: Martin Sheen as Townsend, Dwight Yoakam (also starred in *Sling Blade*), Kyle MacLachlan, Xander Berkley, Kim Greist and Matt Landers. The *Showtime Network* aired Roswell's military drama in the summer of 1994. Videos about the Roswell Incident by Paul Davids, executive producer, include:

> *Roswell*
> *Down in Roswell*
> *Vol. 1 & Vol. 2 (Reply to the*
> *Air Force report on the*
> *Roswell Incident)*

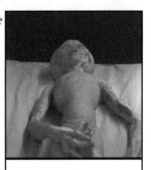

Penthouse Writer Bites on Hoax

Penthouse published an article heralding photos of a real (although dead) alien. The September 1996 issue, their 27th anniversary issue, carried the alien article written by Keith Ferrell.

This alien stirred controversy in Penthouse. A hoaxer sent in some photographs of this alien dummy claiming it to be real.

The story claimed that a German scientist investigated the crash of an alien craft. He gave his daughter the movie film of the alien to prove that the government had covered up the discovery.

The "daughter" remained anonymous in her donation to *Penthouse* because her only interest in releasing the film was furthering the understanding of aliens.

The true source of the photographs soon emerged. Someone had sent *Penthouse* pictures of the alien dummy donated to the International UFO Museum and Research Center (IUFOMRC).

PENTHOUSE Article Spoofed by ALBUQUERQUE JOURNAL Cartoonist

A few days after that *Penthouse* magazine appeared, a cartoon satirizing the alien hoax appeared in the *Albuquerque Journal*. An alien looking at the centerfold of *Penthouse* complains that "they" look like silicone to him.

The Alleged Alien Autopsies

Witnesses to the autopsies, the examinations and the autopsy reports state that the aliens differed from humans in the following ways:
- disproportionately large head and eyes
- a mouth slit with no teeth
- two ear canals on each side of the head, no lobe
- very large four-lobed brain (instead of two-lobed)
- short bone from shoulder to elbow
- unusually long bone from elbow to hand
- four suction-cupped fingers on each hand
- slower metabolism evidenced by large heart and lungs
- tiny circulatory and lymph system combination
- thinner, more flexible bones
- no typical digestive or waste system
- short stature
- unbearable smell

(Randle and Schmitt 1994; Dennis 1991; Corso 1997) These witnesses' stories follow in the Roswell Incident Timeline exhibits.

Controversy Surrounds Roswell Incident

FORBES Writer William Barrett

Unidentified Flying Dollars, July 15, 1996, FORBES.
William Barrett is skeptical about aspects of the Roswell
Incident. Jim Ragsdale, an eyewitness to the alien saucer
crash near Roswell, left doubts in the mind of Barrett. He
questioned Jim Ragsdale's claim about the site of the
crash (see Roswell Timeline pg. 17).

Barrett also mocked the Roswell citizens, claiming
that they have turned the incident into a money maker.
Until Thomas Jennings became mayor in 1994, the
incumbent mayor focused on other aspects of Roswell
rather than the UFO crash. Jennings, however, promoted
Roswell's UFO legacy; he put three space alien dolls in
his office and the official city stationery now bears a flying saucer-shaped watermark.

Barrett claimed that, like Hollywood, Roswell is in the
fantasy business. According to him, people started
remembering bodies, shapes and debris only in the mid-
80s.

Any Single Piece of Evidence Can Be Disputed
Just as Barrett picked Jim Ragsdale's story to dispute,
any single report can be questioned. Even if you throw
out one report, what about the hundreds that remain?

Visitors exploring one of the suspected Roswell crash
sites.

The first few days of
July 1947
would forever change the lives of
those in the small town of
Roswell, New Mexico.
The newspapers said
the Roswell Army Air Field had
captured a flying saucer.
The military would then say
it was just a weather balloon.
What really happened in this
Southeastern New Mexico town?
This is the story from the
individuals whose lives were
changed that July in 1947.

What really happened?
You decide.

CHAPTER 2
Museum Exhibits B & C
The Roswell Incident Timeline

The following exhibits and narratives tell a story about a town thrown into turmoil by the sighting of a flying disc and the crash landing of extraordinary debris and bodies, then further disturbed by an aggressive Army Air Force retrieval and interrogation.

June 24, 1947

A Week Before the Roswell Incident
The Kenneth Arnold Sighting

Kenneth Arnold

HARASSED SAUCER-SIGHTER WOULD LIKE TO ESCAPE FUSS—
PENDLETON, JUNE 28, 1947, UP
KENNETH ARNOLD HAS NOT HAD A MOMENT'S PEACE
SINCE HE REPORTED SEEING NINE FLYING SAUCERS. HE
HAS HAD MANY UNPLEASANT ENCOUNTERS.
...Theories abound. The shiny objects were
new planes or guided missiles in a secret
category. The Army Air Force said if the objects
were moving that fast that they couldn't have
been clocked without radar.
There was another witness to the sighting.
When Arnold landed at Yakima, he talked to another man
that sighted the nine shiny objects from the mountains in
Ukiah. They appeared to dip in and out of formation.

The Mechanix Illustrated
Cover Controversy

Critics of Kenneth Arnold
pointed to the cover illustration of the Navy's
Flapjack Mystery Plane on
Mechanix Illustrated, May
1947: this is where he got
the idea, they said
(FIGURE 1).
However, the Flapjack
Mystery Plane was inca-
pable of going 1700 m.p.h.
Kenneth Arnold clocked
nine objects at 1700
m.p.h., a speed almost
three times faster than that
of any plane known.

FIGURE 1

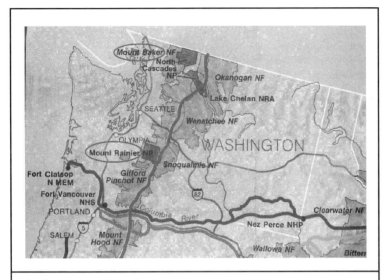

MAP 1

"I could see way off to the right, coming in the vicinity of Mt. Baker, a whole chain-like string of aircraft coming at a tremendous speed."

Kenneth Arnold
pilot and business man

The Kenneth Arnold Story

Watching Nine Crescent-Shaped Discs

Kenneth Arnold, member of the Idaho Search and Rescue Mercy Flyers, cruised toward Mt. Rainier, in Washington state (MAP 1, pg. 11), when he beheld a sight precious to a pilot: A formation of nine aircraft were flying at tremendous speed. He watched intently as they danced in front of him.

Although UFOs have been sighted throughout history, the sighting that began modern media attention started with Arnold, a pilot and business man. On June 24, 1947, Arnold flew over the Cascade mountains searching for a missing Marine Curtiss C-46, a transport plane. In Arnold's words:

> "I had reached the altitude of about 9,200 feet when a very brilliant flash lit the sky around me and actually lit up the airplane that I was flying. I could see way off to the right, coming in the vicinity of Mt. Baker, a whole chain-like string of aircraft coming at a tremendous speed. I could see very plainly that they didn't have any tails. I had never seen aircraft of that kind. And I made a quick first estimate of their speed. The first craft flew at a higher altitude than the last. And, of course, this is completely reversed from our normal flight patterns.
>
> "I had a good fix with Mt. Adams and I thought I'd try to clock their speed between Mt. Rainier and Mt. Adams.

Pretty soon they approached Mt. Adams. I got a good look at them. One particularly, the second from the last one, seemed a little larger and had a definite wraith-like shape, however, when they were flashing and flipping they seemed circular. But as they left the southernmost ridge of Mt. Adams, I looked at my sweep second-hand and they had covered that distance, which is approximately 50 miles, in a minute and forty-two seconds (1700 m.p.h.)."

Arnold lived in Boise, Idaho. He was an accomplished pilot, businessman, law enforcement agent and search and rescue member. He sold firefighting equipment and flew for business and pleasure. Thirty-two years old at the time of the UFO sighting, he was successful and highly respected in his community (Marrs 1997).

Arnold owned his own Cessna airplane. The day of the sighting he flew alone. He had been doing business with Chehailis Central Air Service's chief pilot, Herb Crizner. Crizner told him of the missing marine transport. Arnold, challenged by this, did what he knew best. He took off to find the plane.

Kenneth Arnold getting out of his private plane, a Cessna.

His flight plan took him north of Yakima, Washington. The sighting of the UFOs took less than three minutes. He wasn't upset by the unusual craft; he believed he would receive an explanation when he landed (Randle and Schmitt 1991).

However, he was distracted by the sighting, and after several more minutes of searching, left the area to land. He told the landing crew at Yakima about the sighting, but they were unable to offer any explanation. He then took off for his final destination.

By the time he had landed at Pendleton, Oregon, word had already spread of the incredible sighting. Reporters met him on the ground. It was here that the crafts were given their famous name—flying saucers—meant to describe their movement, not their shape; they were not shaped like saucers, they were crescent-shaped. As Arnold put it: "Bill Bequette, who was a United Press reporter, asked me, 'How do they fly?'

So I told him, 'Well they flew very erratically, like boats on rough water. They would skip, sail, and give off these flashes. You take a saucer and skip it across the water and it's erratic.'

And this is how the name Flying Saucer was born; however, I did not say they were saucer-shaped."

| Flying saucers were given the name by Bill Bequette from the United Press. |

Arnold's sighting proved credible with the press in many areas. Newspapers shrieked the story. The saucers had flown at 1700 mph, three times the known speed of any aircraft able to fly in formation at the time (Berliner and Friedman 1992,1997). Even the military asked for his report.

Introduction to the Roswell Incident

More Than One Saucer May Have Crashed

During the first week of July in 1947, unprecedented reports of crashed flying discs, unusual debris, and aliens dead and alive were reported in southern New Mexico. There are hundreds of civilian and military witnessed who have spoken with investigators about these events (Berlitz and Moore 1980); (Berliner and Friedman 1992,1997); (Randle and Schmitt 1991); (Randle and Schmitt 1994); (Littell 1996).

Apparently at the time of the crashes the military stepped in to do formal retrieval procedures and allegedly threatened many civilians with death if they revealed what they had seen. These traumatic memories were buried for at least 30 years, so when the reports of the events of the first week in July 1947 began to surface in 1978, there was understandably conflicting memories of specific dates. Fortunately, the events occurred around the July 4 holiday, so many witnesses were able to reconstruct the events based on, coincidentally, Independence Day.

There is controversy over the exact location of the crash sites, the dates of the crashes, if there were alien bodies and if any were found alive. Every historical event has opposing scholarly opinion. The Roswell Incident, as it has become known, is no different.

The International UFO Museum and Research Center is committed to providing the raw evidence including the various interpretations of what was seen and experienced by the people in southern New Mexico in July 1947. Some exhibits depict the United States Air Force's conclusions that witnesses saw debris from a Mogul Balloon and crash dummies. In other words, evidence is available for you to make an informed decision for yourself about the events that occurred the first week in July 1947. Our story begins on July 2, 1947...

July 2, 1947

Night of the Storm

The Roswell newspaper, *The Roswell Daily Record*, in its historical story RAAF CAPTURES FLYING SAUCER ON RANCH IN ROSWELL REGION, July 8, 1947, reported that Mr. and Mrs. Dan Wilmot saw a flying disc on the evening of July 2 as it flew through the night sky. They were sitting on their porch when, at about 9:50 P.M., a large glowing object came in from the southeast at a high speed.

> ..[I]heard no sound ...[it was]15 or 20 feet in diameter... [and it]glowed as though light were showing through from inside."
> Dan Wilmot
> —one of the most reliable and respected citizens in town

They got a good look at it after they ran into the yard to watch. It appeared to be 1,500 feet high and careening about 500 miles per hour. The object looked like two saucers mouth to mouth and was estimated to be 15-20 feet in diameter.

The Wilmots watched the disc fly for about 40-50 seconds until it disappeared above the trees near Six-Mile Hill. Mrs. Wilmot heard a swishing sound. Dan Wilmot heard nothing.

The reporter carefully laid a basis for the credibility of the Wilmots' report of the sighting. Wilmot was referred to by the *Record* reporter as one of the most respected and reliable citizens in town, who came forward only after the Army announced they had the saucer. In addition, as with most flying saucer reports, more than one person witnessed the sighting—Dan Wilmot and his wife.

July 4, 1947

The Saucer Crash near Pine Lodge

An explosion rocked Jim Ragsdale and his friend, Trudy Truelove, as they lay in the back of a pickup at about 11:30 P.M. They watched as a 20-foot object crashed through the trees and finally stopped by some rocks sixty yards away. They investigated with flashlights. The object, shaped like a disc, had a big hole torn through the side. They could see inside. Astoundingly, the captain's chair appeared to be made with "rubies and diamonds". (Researchers suggest these may have been glowing light panels.)

> Jim Ragsdale shared this story before he died, July 1, 1995. He had not told anyone since he and Trudy told a few people at a bar the night after the crash. Mysteriously, Trudy died shortly after "they talked" and the debris disappeared from her home and his. He was stunned into silence until many years later when he was diagnosed with cancer. He told his family; they contacted the IUFOMRC. The museum continues to research his claim.

Before Ragsdale and Truelove left in the morning, they went to see the disc in daylight. According to Ragsdale, four little gray bodies lay sprawled in and out of the craft. They picked up pieces of debris and hurriedly left when they heard a siren and saw the military vehicles arriving.

After their weekend date, Truelove went home to Las Cruces with some of the debris. Soon after, she died in an alleged car accident and her share of the debris disappeared. That year, burglars broke into Ragsdale's house and took his debris and his pistol. From that time on he kept quiet out of fear for his life (Littell 1996).

The Nuns at St. Mary's Saw a Fireball

As they watched the fireworks at 11:30 P.M., July 4, 1947, the nuns at St. Mary's hospital saw a mighty fireball falling rapidly through the sky to the northwest. They logged the sight in their log book (Littell 1996).

July 5, 1947*

This fragment of the flying saucer debris is a replica based on witness descriptions. Note the symbols like hieroglyphics in the right upper corner.

Evidence of a Crash—The Debris on Foster Ranch

(East of Corona, New Mexico)

Ranch foreman, William "Mac" Brazel, and his horse-riding pal, 7-year-old Timothy "Dee" Proctor, found some strange metallic debris spread over a hill, down an arroyo and up another hill during the first week in July. The metallic-like pieces were thin and light, but so strong some didn't bend. They could not be cut with a knife or burned with matches. Some unidentifiable type of writings or drawings covered a few pieces.

Brazel and Proctor picked up some of the scrap, unable to stop their rounds for the day. Brazel did not have telephone service on the ranch, so he held on to the scrap until he had a chance to go into town.

Later, when he dropped Dee off, he took it over to show Floyd and Loretta Proctor, Dee's folks. They suggested that he turn it in as proof of flying saucers and receive a reward that was being offered. The Proctors didn't go over to see the debris on the Foster ranch, however, because money for gas was tight and they had chores to do. Mac decided to tell the sheriff about the debris the next time he went into town.

*The date of the Brazel find is not known for certain, other than it took place in the first week in July. Various dates have been given to this important discovery over the years. Some researchers now believe, based on evidence found in the 1990s, that Mac Brazel found the debris on the morning of Friday, July 5, 1947.

July 6, 1947

The Anderson Family—The Plains of San Agustin

One alien was still alive.

Six-year old Gerald Anderson, along with his brother, father, cousin and uncle, found more than they bargained for on their July 6, 1947 rock-hunting trip. First they saw the silvery craft jammed into a hill, then they saw the bodies. Gerald's brother yelled, "Them's Martians." One was alive; one was dying and the other two were dead.

Then Dr. Buskirk, an archaeologist, and his five students came along. Buskirk tried speaking many languages to the being, but to no avail. Barney Barnett, a field engineer for soil conservation, arrived on the scene some time later. Then the military appeared. Gerald Anderson related his story as an adult. He passed a polygraph test in 1991 (Berliner and Friedman 1992,1997).

The San Agustin Plains are 175 miles west of Roswell (MAP 2). Stanton Friedman speculated that the crash may have been caused by two or three saucers colliding, the debris from one saucer landing on Foster Ranch, one landing on the plains of San Agustin and one near Pine Lodge, north of Roswell.

MAP 2
This map shows the San Agustin crash site in relationship to the Corona and Pine Lodge sites.

Crash Site on Corn Ranch

Corn Ranch Ruled Out by Some Investigators and Family

Early in the investigation of the Roswell Incident, an area near Corn Ranch was speculated to be the crash site. This has been ruled out by some researchers of the Roswell Incident. Since Corn Ranch was the first crash site ever to be identified, it quickly grew to fame and is still a popular part of the story of the Roswell Incident. Others believe that the Corn Ranch is a big decoy.

Information from the Affidavit By Jim McKnight 02/02/97

His family has owned the Corn Ranch crash site for three generations. He rode the range on horseback in the area of the alleged crash site in the 1950s.

He questions the validity of the Corn Ranch as a crash site for the following reasons.

1. No one in the family has knowledge of any crash or retrieval.

2. In 1947 there were only 2 places to cross the Macho River on the ranch—5 miles north of the ranch—or through the corrals of the original ranch house, driving southwest along the river, turning north up the bottom, then west up the bank.

3. It is impossible to believe Ragsdale would camp in this area. They never had campers there. People generally go to the mountains for camping.

4. The allegation that some reached the site from Pine Lodge Road is unlikely. One would need to have extensive knowledge of the area to use this access.

5. It was the custom to exchange labor and information among ranching neighbors. They had other military exercises and crashes on the ranch. The Roswell Incident was never discussed.

   "The entire Roswell Incident has been of great interest to me and I hope that we can find the truth someday. I do not have an ax to grind nor a profit to be made from this incident."

                              Jim McKnight

Some Witness Reports on the Crashed Flying Disc, the Aliens and Debris

Witnesses to the Crashed Disc
Jim Ragsdale, civilian
He saw a big flash and heard an explosion that sounded like thunder. An object crashed through trees and stopped between two boulders. It was about 20 feet around. The craft was disc-like with a hole in the side, four feet wide and two feet high. Inside sat a throne-like chair made of "rubies and diamonds." Little people, four feet tall, all dead with skin like a wet snake, lay dead (Littell 1996).

Dr. W. Curry Holden, archaeologist from Texas Tech University
He found a "crashed airplane without wings" with a "fat fuselage" due north of Roswell. He saw three bodies—two outside and one inside—that could be seen from a distance. He didn't enter the craft (Randle and Schmitt 1994). Holden was 92 at the time of his recollection.

Frank Kaufmann, former military man at the site
The craft stuck in the ground at an angle, crushing the front. It had bat-like wings. He found five small beings at the crash site, two outside the craft and three inside. They were not human, but slender with huge heads and large eyes with pupils (Randle and Schmitt 1994).

Major Edwin Easley, Provost Marshall at Roswell
He was responsible for the cordoned area around the 1947 crash. He had seen many crash sites. He stated that the crashed object had not been made on earth, it was extraterrestrial. Then before his death, he also admitted he had seen "the creatures" (Randle and Schmitt 1994). Other researchers claim Easley never revealed what he knew because he had promised not to.

Col. Philip J. Corso, Ret. U.S. Army

Corso came forward at the age of 81 with the information that he encountered the saucer debris and embalmed alien beings during a transit stopover at Fort Riley, Kansas where he was stationed in July 1947. The crates were on their way from Fort Bliss, Texas to Wright Field, Ohio. He looked at one of the aliens in its container. It was a four-foot human-like being with four fingers and a light bulb-shaped head.

Corso, intelligence trained in England, fought in three wars, then later worked at the Pentagon in the Army Research and Development section; ironically he became responsible for the Roswell saucer debris in the early 1960s. He distributed pieces of the Roswell UFO technology into development labs for reverse-engineering, a process of taking an existing technology with an unknown design and making a plan to create it. He and General Trudeau, his superior officer, decided to use the guise that the Roswell debris was smuggled "foreign technology" that needed to be reverse-engineered.

He described some of the debris as: tiny, clear filaments twisted through a harness; 2-inch round gray plastic wafers with wires etched like a map on the surface; colored eye-pieces that illuminated objects seen in the dark to a greenish orange; dull gray metallic-like cloth; a headband with electrode-like devices attached.

He states that the saucer was kept at Edwards Air Force Base in California and that there were alien autopsy reports. The reports described what he had seen: four foot tall human-like aliens with four fingers, thin hands and feet, huge heads, pale gray skin, big almond-shaped eyes, tiny baby-nose that was more like a slit, and a tiny slit mouth (Corso 1997).

Like other witness statements, controversy also besets Corso's statements. Critics point to inconsistencies in the text (the beings had four fingers, Corso states in one place, and six fingers in another) and lack of documented proof of these claims. The critics don't bother Corso, as he says, "I wrote my book for the young people."

Dan Dwyer, Roswell firefighter

Dan saw a triangular-shaped craft and a cloth-like dull-gray metal debris that when folded snapped back to its original shape. The aliens were small, child-like, completely hairless, grayish-brown with a balloon-shaped head. They had large dark eyes, with slits for nose and mouth. Dwyer could feel the helplessness of the creature who lay dying (Randle and Schmitt 1994).

Frankie Dwyer, Dan's daughter

Frankie, a child in 1947, remembers her father letting her play with a piece of the metallic-like cloth. When it was wadded up it returned to its original shape (Randle and Schmitt 1994).

Dr. La June Foster, Spinal Cord Specialist, formerly with the FBI

She stated that one was found alive but died of its injuries. The aliens were short with large heads and strange eyes. Her family confirms her fear of the threats the government made that she would be killed if she revealed what she saw (Randle and Schmitt 1994).

Brigadier General Arthur E. Exon, Air Material Command at Wright-Patterson Air Force Base

B. General Exon was not a Brigadier General in July 1947. He served under Lieutenant General Nathan F. Twining in Air Material Command. He worked with the men who tested the debris coming in from Roswell. He also flew over the crash site and saw the gouge from the "spacecraft" (his word). He also heard there were bodies found outside the craft (Randle and Schmitt 1994).

> *"These people have seen something. What it is I don't know and I am not curious to know."*
> *—Einstein on the UFO flap*

Witnesses' Statements About the Debris Mac Brazel Found

Mac Brazel's original description of the debris does not match any metal known today. Many other witnesses handled that debris and described similar phenomenal properties.

Loretta Proctor, Dee Proctor's mother

She saw the debris when Mac Brazel brought her son home the day of the find. She described the debris as: tan, light, brown and plastic. Both small and large objects could not be cut or burned (Berliner and Friedman 1992,1997).

Bill Brazel, Mac Brazel's son

His description of the material was of a tinfoil-type material similar in weight to balsa, but it couldn't be cut or torn; if it was wrinkled and set down it resumed its original shape—like a metal/plastic. Oddly, sheep would not walk near the debris in the field. Petroglyph-like figures adorned some of the pieces. Army personnel told his father at the time the material was unlike anything the military made (Berliner and Friedman 1992,1997).

While looking over the debris, Bill Brazel may have discovered the wonder of fiber optics (as did Colonel Philip Corso years later in the Pentagon). He found a clear thread-like wire that allowed light to glow from one end and out the other no matter how it was twisted.

Bessie Schreibner, Mac Brazel's daughter

She remembers a metal—like aluminum foil—with some type of tape that could not be removed. It was covered with lettering and numbers like Japanese written in columns. A second piece she recalls looked like a pipe sleeve, other pieces like heavily waxed paper (Berliner and Friedman 1992,1997).

Major Jesse A. Marcel, Intelligence Officer

He recalled the debris as paper thin, strong enough to be hit with a sledgehammer without denting the thin foil material. The I-beams had the weight of balsa but were a metallic/plastic-like material that would not burn. He found no trace of radioactivity on them.

Jesse Marcel, Jr. MD, Major Marcel's son

He has been instrumental in having replicas of the debris manufactured. He knows that the I-beam piece had hieroglyphic writing—in violet with a metallic hue on it; other plain, thin, lead pieces were as light as a feather. A few years after he saw the debris from the crash he became an avid model builder; he knows the debris was not balsa wood and paper.

Controversies About Witnesses' Statements

Every witness to the crashed disc, aliens and debris has had their testimony (and their character) reviewed by many researchers. Every witness statement has been challenged and many of them are discounted by one researcher or another, to this day. The dates, the sites and some of the descriptions vary, although slightly.

One thing is certain: odd crashes occurred in southern New Mexico during the first week in July 1947. Many credible sources have laid their reputations on the line admitting they saw what they believed was something and some beings not from this earth. Many of these witnesses had knowledge of the most highly technical devices available in 1947.

Some researchers have taken a psychological approach to the differences in accounts and propose that this is how myths are created (Saler, Ziegler and Moore 1997), (Thompson 1991). Saler, Ziegler and Moore in their work for the Smithsonian Institution particularly point to the changes in the story as it has unfolded over time. Ironically, their research may point to a very important discovery about our ancient myths. Do we refer to stories about these beings as myths wherever we find them?

Also On July 6, 1947

Sheriff George A. Wilcox and Family is Threatened

Mac Brazel came into town on July 6 to show Sheriff Wilcox the debris he found on the ranch near Corona. Sheriff Wilcox didn't recognize this extraordinary material, so he called Major Jesse Marcel, intelligence officer at the Roswell Army Air Force (RAAF) base.

Marcel took over immediately, but then Wilcox had difficulty getting any follow-up information from the army. Sheriff Wilcox may have gone out to the ranch to get more information and found it cordoned off by the military.

On July 8, under orders from Col. Blanchard, Lt. Walter Haut sent a press release out at noon that the military had recovered a flying disc. The sheriff's office was deluged with calls.

On July 9 several military men arrived in Wilcox's office and demanded the remaining debris brought in by Brazel be returned to them. Before leaving, the military police threatened to kill Sheriff Wilcox, his wife, Inez, and their family if they told anyone about the debris.

Sheriff Wilcox did not run for re-election.

> ## If They Told They Would Be Killed
>
> George Wilcox's granddaughter, Barbara, said her grandmother, Inez, told her, "When the [Roswell] incident happened, the military police came to the jailhouse and told George and I that if we ever told anything about the incident, not only would we be killed, but our entire family would be killed."

July 7, 1947

The Military Called the Mortician
Glenn Dennis' Eyewitness Story
(Co-Founder of the Museum and Research Center)

Glenn Dennis received some unusual phone calls from the army base on July 7,1947. The Mortuary Officer at the RAAF base first called to ask Dennis about the availability of a number of four-foot caskets. Naturally, Dennis was very concerned about the deaths of any military children and asked what happened, but he was told the caskets were for "future planning."

Less than an hour later, the officer called back and asked a number of unusual questions about embalming fluid and preserving bodies found outside after being exposed for some time. Dennis answered his questions and offered to do the embalming for the Army according to their specifications, but nothing came of his offer.

Dennis also ran the ambulance service with his hearse. He had to drive a serviceman with a head injury out to the base a short time after the phone calls. As he walked to the infirmary, he saw debris— stainless steel shaded from pink to red to brown then black—in and around three old army field ambulances. He saw hieroglyphic markings on the edge of one piece that reminded him of Egyptian decorations he had studied about in his embalming class in mortuary school.

The military personnel reacted with surprise and anger when he entered the infirmary. They tried to order him out by claiming he would make up rumors about what he saw (Dennis 1991).

Then a nurse he knew ran into the hall and protectively screamed through her sobs for Dennis to get out as fast as he could.

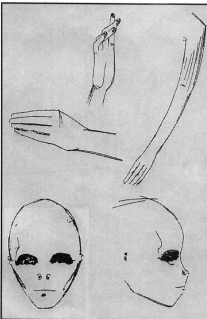

These drawings by Glenn Dennis reproduce the drawings the nurse made for him in July 1947 (Dennis 1991).

The nurse met Glenn later at the officers' club. She appeared to be in shock. She cried as she spoke. She grew up in a protective mid-west American family. She had gone to all Catholic schools and was away from home for the first time. She planned to return to the Catholic order after her tour of duty. Young and innocent, she was hardly prepared for the job she had performed that day.

She told Glenn she came upon two fully gowned doctors standing over two tiny bodies in bags. They asked her to take notes. She did not know the doctors, but took the notes.

She described the little beings to Dennis and gave him pictures she had drawn on the back of prescription notes. After that night, Dennis never heard from her again despite his many efforts to make contact. When he tried to reach her at the base the next day, he was told she had been transferred to England. Eventually, that year, he received a letter he'd sent her overseas returned and stamped "return to sender" and "deceased" (Dennis 1991). The nurse asked Glenn never to reveal her name so he has withheld her name to this day.

Major Marcel Handles The Saucer Debris

Major Jesse Marcel Brings Debris Home

After finishing a day of debris clean-up at Foster Ranch, Major Jesse Marcel brought the unique debris home to show his wife and 11-year old son. The family spread the debris out on the kitchen floor. Marcel's son, Jesse Jr., spotted the I-Beam with the unusual violet symbols that lined the inner surface on one side of the slim piece.

Photographer-Miller Johnson

I-Beam Replica—Donated by Miller Johnson, industrial designer 1995. Made in collaboration with Dr. Jesse Marcel Jr.and Kent Jeffrey, pilot.

They examined the other pieces of fascinating debris. The metal was like thin lead foil—light as feathers—and the plastic-type pieces resembled Bakelite™. Major Marcel told them the pieces came from a flying saucer. Young Jesse Jr. had never heard of flying saucers before.

The I-Beam Replica Project

Miller Johnson, an industrial designer, met museum co-founders, Glenn Dennis and Walter Haut, along with Max Littell, IUFOMRC business consultant, at a ceremony to dedicate a plaque to the founding 100 members of the Museum. Johnson proposed a plan to replicate the I-beam that witnesses had described from the Roswell crash. The museum officers liked the idea and encouraged Johnson to go ahead.

Kent Jeffrey contacted Johnson a short time later with a similar plan. So they collaborated on the project with Dr. Jesse Marcel, Jr. First, Marcel drew the characters on the I-beam as he recalled them and found the correct lavender color in the Pantone Matching System, the color system graphic designers use.

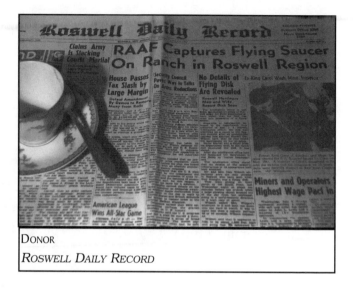

DONOR

ROSWELL DAILY RECORD

July 8, 1947

Press Release written by Lt. Walter Haut
(Co-Founder of the International UFO Museum and
Research Center)
A Headline That Went Around the World.
RAAF Captures Flying Saucer On Ranch in Roswell Region
NO DETAILS OF FLYING DISK ARE REVEALED
ROSWELL HARDWARE MAN AND WIFE REPORT DISK SEEN
The intelligence office of the 509th Bombardment
group at Roswell Army Air Field announced at noon
today that the field has come into possession of a
flying saucer.

According to information released by the
department, over authority of Maj. J. A. Marcel,
intelligence officer, the disk was recovered on a
ranch in the Roswell vicinity, after an unidentified
rancher had notified Sheriff Geo. Wilcox, here, that
he had found the instrument on the premises...
(*Roswell Daily Record 1947*).

Also on July 8, 1947

It's Just a Weather Balloon

General Ramey changed the Army Air Force's story when Major Marcel arrived in Fort Worth, Texas with the cartons of debris. He and Marcel sat surrounded by the debris Marcel had retrieved from Brazel's ranch. Then Ramey took Marcel into another room. When they returned the debris was gone! It had been replaced by wreckage from a weather balloon.

> ...the debris was gone! It had been replaced by wreckage from a weather balloon.

Ramey briefed Marcel for the press conference. He ordered Marcel to remain quiet. Then Ramey made a fool of Marcel in front of the press for confusing a flying disk with a weather balloon.

Col. Thomas DuBose, General Ramey's Chief of Staff, later confirmed that the weather balloon story covered up the true origin of the debris which had become top secret.

The military personnel at Roswell, under orders from Washington D.C., kept Major Marcel in the dark when he returned on July 9.

He received no further official information about the debris.

Admiral Roscoe H. Heillenkoetter, Third Director of the CIA, Allegedly a Member of Majestic-12

From the NEW YORK TIMES, February 28, 1960

"Through official secrecy and ridicule, many citizens are led to believe that unidentified flying objects are nonsense. To hide the facts the Air Force has silenced its personnel."

The Radio Broadcast and The Aborted Interview

Whitmore's Interview of a Lifetime

Frank Joyce worked at the KGFL radio station in Roswell. He heard about the debris Brazel found on Foster ranch first at the station (Berliner and Friedman 1992,1997).

Later Joyce told his boss, Walt Whitmore Sr., owner of the radio station, about the debris Brazel had found. Whitmore went out to find Brazel. Whitmore and Brazel went to Whitmore's home for the night to record the exclusive interview (Littell 1996).

The next morning Whitmore was stopped cold by a government official in Washington before the tape could air. The official reminded Whitmore he needed an FCC license to operate his radio station and he would lose it if he aired any interview with Mac Brazel. No one saved the recording.

Whitmore's son, Walter E. Whitmore Jr. remembers the incident well. He came home to spend the July 4th weekend with his family and Mac Brazel was staying in his room (Littell 1996).

Radio Station Broadcasting Booth Exhibit

Where the News of a Crashed Flying Disc Never Stops
Complete with a teletype, telephone, and typewriter from
the 1947 time period, this radio station continuously
plays a reproduced newscast from American Broad-
casting Company that would stun the world: The army
recovered pieces of a crashed flying disc.

Walt Whitmore Sr. tried to follow up on this story,
as stated earlier, by interviewing Mac Brazel, who found
debris on Foster Ranch. They didn't do the interview live,
but recorded it and unfortunately didn't finish until after
10 P.M. that night. By that time, KGFL had signed off the
air for the night. He never got to play the recorded interview before he received the threats that he might lose his
FCC license if he put the Brazel interview on the air. It is
believed that Whitmore used a wire recording device for
the interview (Randle and Schmitt 1994).

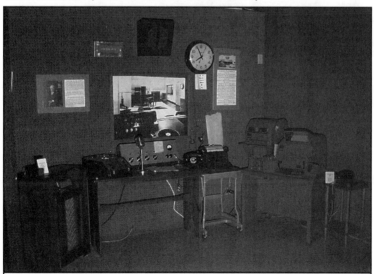

Radio Room Exhibit
DONOR
Bob Barnes

Interrupted Transmission

As Lydia Sleppy was sending the message shown to the right, she received an interrupt message.

The Teletype Message U.S. Citizens Never Received Roswell, NM "One of those mysterious flying disks has crashed on a ranch north of Roswell, New Mexico and soldiers from U.S. Army Air Force have been dispatched to recover the object. According to our reporter at the scene the objects look like a giant dishpan badly damaged on one edge from the impact with the ground. There are also reports of the bodies of small cre..." [Lydia Sleppy came to this line when her transmission was interrupted by bells (Berliner and Friedman 1992,1997).] This message followed:

LLLINE INTERRUPT ***BELLS***
Attention ABQ,
CEASE TRANSMISSION IMMEDIATELY

Do not transmit this story

Authority FBI, Dallas, TX
070547.996277
BELLS

*Teletype bells rang when transmissions began and ended.

July 8, 1947
The Army Takes Brazel Into Custody

Brazel was taken by the army when they found him— that night the military personnel escorted him to town and stood by while he told a new story about his discovery to reporters and Frank Joyce, from the radio station. Months later he moved away.

Army Air Force men escorted Mac Brazel to the base on July 8. Military officials kept him in a small house and did not allow anyone except authorized military personnel to speak to him. No one knows what the military said to Brazel; but that night, the military escorted Brazel to the newspaper and to the radio station. They listened while he told reporters and Frank Joyce a story about finding wreckage on June 16 and that it was ordinary rubber and other materials familiar to him.

The military then escorted him back to the base and kept him for seven days. Brazel could not even contact his wife or son. He angrily told friends later that he was badly treated by the military.

And he never again told anyone anything about the debris (Randle and Schmitt 1994).

Harassed Rancher who Located 'Saucer' Sorry He Told About It

Mac Brazel Regrets that He Told About the Debris
Headline from a story in the ROSWELL DAILY RECORD
July 9, 1947.

Summary of Events June/July 1947

June 24
Kenneth Arnold sights nine discs in Washington State
flying in formation at approximately 1700 m.p.h.

July 2
Wilmots see a flying disc over Roswell.

July 4
Jim Ragsdale and Trudy Truelove watch a disc crash
near Pine Lodge.
Nuns at a hospital in Roswell see a fireball crashing in
the northwest.

July 5
Military begins retrieval of a disc at the Pine Lodge crash
site.
Mac Brazel and Dee Proctor find debris on Foster Ranch.

July 6
Brazel takes debris to Sheriff Wilcox and is interviewed
by Walt Whitmore of the KGFL radio station.
Gerald Anderson, his family and others find a saucer
with a live alien, one dying, and two dead ones near San
Agustin.

July 7
Glenn Dennis sees debris at RAAF base hospital and
meets with a nurse who observed an alien examination.
Major Marcel picks up debris on Foster ranch then
Jesse Marcel Jr.,11, handles the debris at home.

July 8
Lt. Walter Haut sends press release: Army Recovers Disk.
General Ramey orders Marcel to identify debris as a
weather balloon during Ft. Worth press conference.
Mac Brazel tells a new story after Army holds him.

What Happened to Major Marcel?

Major Marcel Was Promoted

Instead of being severely reprimanded by his superiors, and demoted for what would have been an enormous blunder if he had mistaken a weather balloon (or a Mogul balloon) for a flying saucer, Marcel was promoted to Lieutenant Colonel. If he had made an error of that magnitude, his military career would have been finished.

Although the Army forced him to recant his statement during the press conference in Ft. Worth, July 8, 1947, during interviews with William Moore and Stanton Friedman in 1979, Marcel stated that he was "acquainted with virtually every type of weather-observation or radar tracking device being used by either the civilians or the military" (Berlitz and Moore 1980). He simply said what he found in the scrub desert on the Foster ranch was nothing we made.

One final important piece of information. Major Marcel clearly said on a number of occasions that the hieroglyphic-type writing was unfamiliar to him, but he knew it meant something. This is important to bear in mind when examining the tape on the balsa wood frame attached to the Mogul balloon (see page 42, FIGURE 2). The tape bears random drawings of shapes familiar to humans and would have been recognized as such by Major Marcel.

> The I-Beams had little symbols Marcel called hieroglyphics because he could not interpret them. He knew they meant something and they were not all the same (Berliner and Friedman 1992, 1997).

Newspaper Clippings Around the U. S. July 1947

DALLAS MORNING NEWS— DALLAS, TX 7/8/47

Clearwater Merchants Organize Hunt for Flying Disks

Wm. Rehbaum and Robert Workman of Clearwater Flying Co. in conjunction with radio station WCLE searched for disks with planes and armed crews. They described disks as Plexiglas-domed circular planes.

BOSTON AMERICAN BOSTON, MA

FBI PROBES FLYING DISKS

Harvard Experts say "We're Puzzled"

PRESS HAROLD PORTLAND, ME 7/7/47

British Compare Flying Saucers With Own Loch Ness Monster

"Believe They Will Go Away If Yanks Take Pledge and Stiff Drink of Soda"

By: Ed Creagh London, 7/6/47 (AP)

The British are reacting to news of flying saucers with tongue in cheek. They make an interesting comparison to stories of rockets seen in Sweden between July and October, 1946.

Mystery Flying Disks
Reported in 31 States

**BOSTON DAILY RECORD
—BOSTON, MA 7/5/47**

Flying Disks
Put On A Wild
Holiday Show

There have been reported sightings by residents in Portland and Eugene, OR and Van Couver, WA.

GAZETTE
TAUNTON (TOWNTON), MA
7/5/47

Flying Saucer Tales Continue

More Are Seen

Portland, OR 7/5/47 (AP)

Flying Saucer Story Reaches Fever Pitch

"I saw them myself" states a veteran United Airline crew member. One seen by scores of Portland residents. Another by 60 picnickers at Twin Falls, ID park. Others seen by police and 3 newspaper men. In New Orleans, Lillian Lawless saw a shining object flying at great height and terrific speed over Lake Ponchartrain.

PRESS
HERALD
PORT-
LAND, ME
7/7/47

**Army
Planes
Comb Skies
For Flying
Craft Carry
Cameras But
Fail in Hunt
Jet Fighter
Kept Ready to
Take Off**

San Francisco,
July 6 (AP)

Newspaper Clippings Tell All

NY HERALD TRIBUNE
NEW YORK, NY 7/10/47

Flying Disks Now Vanishing Into Thin Air

Reports of their Sighting are Falling Off; Army Rebukes Roswell Officers

The reports of flying disks which have been coming in since June 25 have almost stopped.

In Washington the United press said Army AF Headquarters was reported to have delivered a strong rebuke to officers at the Roswell, NM Army Air Base. The officers announced on Tuesday "that a flying disk had been found there." The disk created a stir, but finally was identified as an old weather balloon. The rancher who found it on the desert said he was sorry he had anything to do with it.

HERALD JOURNAL
LOGAN, UT 7/11/47

Saucers in the Sky so Numerous They're a Dime a Dozen

Army officials believe that the saucers are hoaxes and the sightings are caused by hysteria. Two college students in Lillington, NC reported a bright light 10 miles from Raleigh at 11:45 P.M. yesterday. "It moved in circular orbit and appeared to be an elliptical shape with blue lights radiating from it, mostly around the edges." It vanished when they drove towards it. They watched it for 3 minutes.

Museum visitor Thomas See examines the evidence at the Mogul Balloon Exhibit.

CHAPTER 3
Museum Exhibit D
The Great Coverup
Mogul Balloon Story
Roswell Report: Case Closed

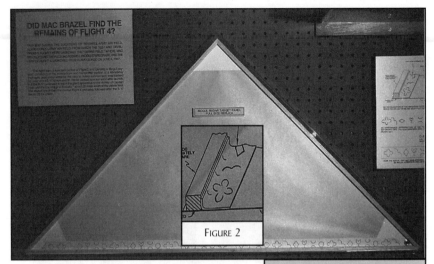

FIGURE 2

Project Mogul

Since 1994 the Air Force Has Claimed Mac Brazel Found Debris from a Mogul Balloon Train

Mogul was a code name for a program to detect and monitor Soviet nuclear weapons. A team at New York University College of Engineering designed and tested the balloons under a contract with the military. The U.S. Army Air Force used the balloon system to detect sound waves made by atomic blasts. The system consisted of acoustical sensors, radar reflecting targets, parachutes, and weather balloons constructed of aluminized paper glued and taped to a balsa wood frame (figure 2). The balloon train only weighed 63 pounds. The first balloon was launched on June, 4 1947 from Alamagordo Army Airfield, N.M. (McAndrew 1997).

Charles B. Moore discovered the use of polyethylene for high altitude balloon construction, which was used for Mogul. It is a lightweight plastic widely used today.

Project Mogul Display
DONORS & CREATORS
Miller Johnson—designed and fabricated the exhibit and models. The text was written by Karl T. Pflock, Writer and UFO Researcher. All technical data was supplied by Professor Charles B. Moore.

Operation Majestic-12
Special Classified Executive Order of Harry Truman
President of the United States 1947

The Great Coverup

Majestic-12 was identified as "a top secret" Research and Development/Intelligence operation, twelve men who answered only to the President. They consulted with Presidents Truman and Eisenhower on the profound questions presented by the discovery of UFOs.

Majestic-12 (MJ-12) conjures up visions of a royal court. In the late 40s and early 50s this extraordinary group of men amounted to the equivalent. Composed of top-notch scientists, intelligence officers and representatives from all branches of the armed services, this team prepared a brief to update the newly elected President Eisenhower (Friedman 1996,1997).

How the Existence of Majestic-12 Was Discovered

The Majestic-12 documents were delivered anonymously on a roll of undeveloped film in December 1984 to Jaime Shandera a movie director working on a fictional UFO story. Eight pages of documents entitled *Briefing Document: Operation Majestic-12 Prepared for President-Elect Dwight D. Eisenhower: (Eyes Only) 18 November 1952*. The briefing recounted the recovery of a crashed flying saucer and four alien bodies northwest of Roswell in early July 1947. There were strange symbols on the wreckage and the bodies were not *homo sapiens*. Majestic-12 was established in September 1947 to study and evaluate these findings (Friedman 1996).

Controversy has raged ever since about the authenticity of the documents. As of the date of this printing, fourteen years later, these documents have not been proven to be forgeries. Stanton Friedman has done extensive research on the documents and, based on visits to 18 archives, is convinced that some are genuine.

Lee Graham Takes MJ-12 Document Authenticity Question Back to the Government

As an Aerojet company researcher, Lee Graham signed a secret security agreement regarding disclosure of top secrets. When he came into possession of the MJ-12 documents, he sent a report to the Vice President of the U.S.A. stating that top security information might have been compromised by the disclosure of MJ-12 documents. He received a letter from the Defense Investigative Service along with copies of the MJ-12 documents marked UNCLASSIFIED. Dale Hartig, Defense Investigative Service agent, clarified later in writing that the MJ-12 documents were genuine (Marrs 1997).

According to the Documents—The Men of MJ-12

The Scientists

Four men provided the technical and scientific information necessary to evaluate the UFO ships, their inhabitants, their technical capabilities and origins: Lloyd Berkner; scientific leader of the space program, Dr. Jerome Hunsaker; aeronautical engineer at MIT, Dr. Donald Menzel, astronomer at Harvard; and Dr. Detlev Bronk, aviation physiologist, chair of the National Academy of Sciences. One man, Dr. Vannevar Bush, a research and development leader, had the interesting job of finding people to reverse-engineer the UFO technology.

The Intelligence Officers

The perceived threat from the UFOs was serious enough, but the government also faced the threat of UFO technology falling into the hands of foreign governments. After all, the astounding technology had literally fallen into the hands of the U.S. government.

Gordon Gray, former Secretary of the Army, and Sidney Souers, first director of the CIA, served as the eyes and ears for Majestic-12 in the international arena.

Armed Services-Our Brightest and Best

James Forrestal, Secretary of the Navy and first Secretary of Defense, was the most troubled of the MJ-12 group, whether by the UFO events, no one knows for certain. He was admitted to a hospital where he eventually committed suicide by jumping backwards out of a 16th floor window in May 1949 (Spencer 1991); (Vallee 1991); (Andrews 1993).

> James Forrestal committed suicide. Did the pressure of responsibility for the safety of the American people push him over the edge?

Other military leaders in MJ-12 included General Hoyt Vandenberg, Air Force Vice Chief of Staff; General Nathan Twining, Head of Air Material Command later to become Head of the Joint Chiefs of Staff; General Walter Smith, Fourth Director of the CIA; and General Robert M. Montague, Army, Head of Fort Bliss.

Stanton Friedman, nuclear physicist, has documented his research into the authenticity of this MJ-12 organization in his book, *Top Secret/Majic*. The Great Coverup—Museum Exhibit D is adapted from that work.

> General Twining, head of Air Material Command wrote in a memo to the Commanding General Army Air Forces, Brig. General George Schulgen, Sept. 23, 1947: "... presented below is the considered opinion of this Command concerning the so-called "Flying Discs."
> ..."The phenomenon reported is something real not visionary or fictitious.
> ..."There are objects probably approximating the shape of a disc, of such appreciable size as to appear to be as large as man-made aircraft."
> January 1969 Condon Report (Friedman 1996,1997)

A-8

TOP SECRET

EYES ONLY

THE WHITE HOUSE

WASHINGTON

September 24, 1947.

MEMORANDUM FOR THE SECRETARY OF DEFENSE

Dear Secretary Forrestal:

As per our recent conversation on this matter, you are hereby authorized to proceed with all due speed and caution upon your undertaking. Hereafter this matter shall be referred to only as Operation Majestic Twelve.

It continues to be my feeling that any future considerations relative to the ultimate disposition of this matter should rest solely with the Office of the President following appropriate discussions with yourself, Dr. Bush and the Director of Central Intelligence.

Harry Truman

TOP SECRET EYES ONLY   THE WHITE HOUSE

September 24, 1947

MEMORANDUM FOR THE SECRETARY OF DEFENSE

Dear Secretary Forrestal:

As per our recent conversation on this matter, you are hereby authorized to proceed with all due speed and caution upon your undertaking. Hereafter this matter shall be referred to only as Operation Majestic Twelve.

It continues to be my feeling that any future consideration relative to the ultimate disposition of this matter should rest solely with the Office of the President following appropriate discussions with yourself, Dr. Bush and the Director of Central Intelligence.

Harry Truman

J. Edgar Hoover Didn't Get to See It
July 10, 1947

Background

The Air Force and the FBI squabbled over who would do the follow-up work on UFO reports. Army Air Force General Schulgen asked the FBI for help in completing investigations (Shawcross 1997). The following note circulated within the FBI with four people writing on it.

Memorandum for Mr. Ladd

     Mr. [blackened out] also discussed this matter with Colonel L. R. Forney of [illegible]. Colonel Forney indicated that it was his attitude that inasmuch as it has been established that the flying disks are not the result of any Army or Navy experiments, the matter is of interest to the FBI. He stated that he was of the opinion that the Bureau, if at all possible, should accede to General Schulgen's request.
SWR:AJB

ADDENDUM

I would recommend that we advise the Army that the Bureau does not believe it should go into these investigations, it being noted that the great bulk of those alleged discs reported found have been pranks. It is not believed that the Bureau would accomplish anything by going into these investigations.
     DEL [Ladd]

(Clyde Tolson) [handwriting]
I think we should do this. 7-15 [1947]

(J. Edgar Hoover) [handwriting]
I would do it but before agreeing to it we must insist upon full access to discs recovered. For instance in the [illegible] case the army grabbed it and would not let us have it for cursory examination.   H.
(Randle and Schmitt 1994)

The date corresponds with the Roswell Incident.

What The Air Force Claims Crashed in Roswell

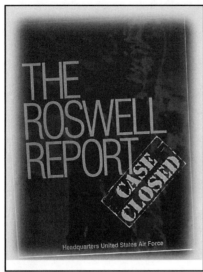

Excerpts From THE
ROSWELL REPORT: CASE
CLOSED 1997
Headquarters United States Air Force

From the Foreword
by Secretary of the Air
Force, Sheila E. Widnall
The "Roswell incident"
has assumed a central
place in American folk-
lore. My objective is simple and consistent: to find
all the facts and bring
them to light.

The Author
Capt. James McAndrew, Intelligence Applications Officer,
the Pentagon, Washington, DC., co-author of *Roswell
Report: Fact vs. Fiction in the New Mexico Desert* (1995).

Introduction
A July 1994 Air Force (AF) report was 1000 pages. The
information it included was: The Army AF recovered
material near Roswell in July 1947. The debris came
from an Army AF balloon-borne research project code
named Mogul. That report didn't discuss "bodies"
because none were involved, according to the report.

Subsequent to the 1994 report, USAF researchers
discovered information providing a rational explanation.
"It appears that UFO proponents have failed to establish
the accurate dates for these alien observations (in some
instances by more than a decade)." The USAF claims
that Roswell witnesses' reports of finding unusual bodies
are reports erroneously connected to a Mogul crash.

Air Force Conclusions from Additional Research Since 1994

1. AF activities which occurred over many years were consolidated by witnesses and are now represented as having happened in 2 or 3 days in July 1947.

2. Aliens were probably anthropomorphic test dummies that were carried aloft by a USAF high altitude balloon for scientific research.

3. "Unusual" military activities in the New Mexico desert were balloon launch and recovery operations. The reports of military units arriving shortly after "UFO" crashes were accurate descriptions of AF personnel engaged in dummy retrieval.

Close-up of an anthropomorphic crash dummy face.

4. Claims of bodies at the Roswell Army Air Field hospital were most likely combinations of 2 separate incidents:

a. "a 1956 KC-97 aircraft accident killing 11 AF members.

b. "a 1959 manned balloon mishap which injured 2 AF pilots.

"This report is based on thoroughly documented research supported by official records, technical reports, film footage,
photographs, and interviews with individuals who were involved in these events."

Excerpts from Text of THE ROSWELL REPORT: CASE CLOSED

pg.19 "Dummy Joe" made more than 5000 jumps between 1918-1924. Dummy testing continued with parachute jump tests through WW II.

pg. 21 "In 1949 a contract was awarded to Sierra Engineering Company of Sierra Madre, CA, and deliveries began in 1950. This dummy quickly became known as 'Sierra Sam'."

pg. 23 High altitude balloon drops were done from 1953-1959, six years after the Roswell Incident. Some of the drops were in the areas where the "crashed saucer" and "space aliens" were allegedly observed.

pg. 30 Recovery of test dummies by personnel from Holloman AFB Balloon Branch. From 8-12 recovery personnel arrived as soon as possible following the impact of an anthropomorphic dummy (1956-1959).

pg. 33 Dummies were not always recovered immediately, or at all. Dummies and instrumentation were often damaged from impact. Loss of heads and limbs and fingers was not uncommon: *"This detail, dummies with missing fingers, appears to satisfy another element of the research profile—aliens with only four fingers."*

Some Questions Unanswered by THE ROSWELL REPORT: CASE CLOSED

•What exploded?

•What gouged the earth?

•Why didn't any of the materials burn?

•Why were two doctors performing examinations on crash dummies at the RAAF base infirmary?

•The anthropomorphic (human-like) dummies the Air Force described were that of six ft. tall, 190-pound dummies not used until May 1953. Why do people remember little bodies in 1947?

•Why did the military request four foot coffins on July 7, 1947 for future planning?

•Why didn't Major Marcel recognize balsa wood?

"Why indeed, Scully," Mulder might ask. (TV characters from the X-Files on Fox Network.)

pg. 35 Holloman AFB used wooden shipping containers similar to coffins. Dummy manufacturers recommended canvas stretchers and hospital gurneys as modes of transport. The first 10 dummy drops used black or silver insulation bags, similar to "body bags" in which dummies were placed for flight to guard against equipment failure at low ambient temperatures of the upper atmosphere.

High Altitude Balloon Operations

pg. 37 Many balloons launched from Holloman AFB were recovered under circumstances and in locations that strongly resembled those described by UFO proponents. The First High Altitude Balloon was launched on June 4, 1947 and was found by a rancher.

ROSWELL REPORT: CASE CLOSED — For sale by the Superintendent of Documents, U.S. Government Printing Office, Washington, D.C. 20402 cost: $18.00

Retired Lt. Col. Raymond A. Madson, formerly with the crash test dummy program, said he's not buying the latest Air Force explanation of what occurred in Roswell.

Only Two High Altitude Balloon Dummies Dropped Near Roswell

Out of 43 dummies launched from Holloman AFB, N.M. only 2 landed near Roswell: on 11/17/55 and 10/8/57.

Introducing the U.S. Air Force's Anthropomorphic Dummy "HAROLD-serial no. 226 ". Sierra Sam design by Alderson Labs used from 1952 to the late 1960s. HAROLD is on loan from the Space Center in Alamogordo, New Mexico.

Museum Exhibit of Anthropomorphic Crash Dummy
Loaned by—International Space Hall of Fame

The Air Force claims that witnesses to the Roswell Incident, who include trained emergency personnel, medical practitioners and enlisted soldiers, mistook these 6 feet tall, 190 pound dummies for space aliens and confused the dates they saw them by 10 years. ROSWELL REPORT: CASE CLOSED has motivated many people to visit the IUFOMRC.

Nuclear Physicist Stanton Friedman's Analysis of the Air Force's Reports on Roswell

It's Propaganda

The 1994, *The Roswell Report: Fact vs. Fiction in the New Mexico Desert* by USAF Colonel Richard Weaver and the 1997, *Roswell Report: CASE CLOSED* are text book examples of propaganda, Friedman states in his written analysis. They contain selective choice of data, errors of omission, intentional deception and inconsistency with the truth. Friedman has been interviewing Roswell Incident witnesses since 1978.

One point that cannot be stressed too strongly is that the army personnel like Major Jesse Marcel involved in this incident were from the 509th Bomb Group that were the only men trained to drop "the bomb." And, in fact, they did drop the atomic bombs on Japan. These men were considered by the armed services to be impeccable soldiers. And this crashed flying disc discovery was coincident with the over 1000 UFO sightings preceding the Roswell Incident.

The news release put out by Lt. Walter Haut was done under the authority of Colonel William Blanchard. Blanchard presumably would have looked at the findings for himself, given its importance. Then Brigadier General Roger Ramey, Blanchard's boss, issued a statement that the debris was from a weather balloon. Ramey's chief of staff, Colonel Thomas Jefferson DuBose, swore in a 1980 statement that Ramey received a call from General Clements in Washington D.C. to cover up the crashed flying disc story.

Discrepancies in the Air Force Report and Friedman's Findings

The Air Force claims that what was recovered in Roswell was found on June 14, 1947 and was a debris bundle consisting of tinfoil, paper, tape and sticks about 18-20

inches long and 7 or 8 inches thick, weighing about 5 pounds. There were letters on some parts and tape with flowers printed on it. No strings or wires were found.

Friedman points out that the absence of strings and wires is significant. The strings and wires were a considerable part of a Mogul balloon train. Also, *The Roswell Daily Record* reported on July 8 that Brazel found the wreckage "last week." This does not coincide with the AF date of June 14. Bill Brazel, Loretta Proctor and Dr. Jesse Marcel Jr. are all still alive and have handled the material that was found and they were not mentioned in the index of the AF reports. Then, it is inconceivable that Major Marcel would drive over many miles of hot and dusty roads in the middle of summer in southern New Mexico, back to Brazel's field, when the pile of debris would have fit in Brazel's truck. Colonel Jesse Marcel stated that the strewn wreckage was hundreds of yards long.

In addition, note that Mac Brazel had recovered 2 weather balloons before this debris fell on Foster Ranch and that was not mentioned in the Air Force reports. Weather balloons were part of the Mogul balloon train.

Friedman also interviewed Lt. Colonel Raymond Madson about the crash test dummy program. He and his wife stated that while they were working in the early 1950s at Wright Patterson Air Force Base, they heard separate stories of small strange bodies having been brought there years earlier.

Friedman's Explanation of the Air Force's Approach

1. The USAF has been lying about Roswell for years, to everyone. It works!
2. The USAF doesn't care what people think of the USAF explanations as long as the media buys it.
3. USAF's second report tried to explain "the bodies" after Colonel Weaver stated there didn't need to be a consideration of bodies since the Mogul balloon didn't carry bodies.
4. A UFO proponent infiltrated the Air Force and did the report to discredit the Air Force's Roswell explanation.

THE ROSWELL DAILY RECORD carries the story of the 1997 Air Force Report,
THE ROSWELL REPORT: CASE CLOSED 1997, and the reactions of the co-
founders of the IUFOMRC, Walter Haut (large photo) and Glenn Dennis
(top small photo), as well as Deon Crosby (small bottom photo),
IUFOMRC's director. Walter displays here the original stories that were
printed by the ROSWELL DAILY RECORD at the time of the crash. He sent out
the original press release that stated that the army recovered a flying disc.

THE DAY AFTER ROSWELL Also Published in 1997

A Retired Colonel from the U.S. Army Tells a Story Different Than the Air Force Reports

Colonel Philip Corso, retired, worked in Army Research and Development at the Pentagon in the 50s and 60s. He says that the Roswell saucer-crash debris was divided up among the branches of the armed services. The R & D from the Army alone has provided us with: integrated circuits, fiber optics, lasers, night vision goggles, irradiated food, super-strong fibers, headband guidance systems, particle beams, kevlar vests and electromagnetic propulsion systems. These items are consistent with what witnesses to the Roswell Incident debris claimed to have seen.

A Word in Defense of What the Army Did in 1947

"Many people have criticized the army and the government for maintaining the Roswell cover-up not only at the time but also through the years. For that I need to say a word in defense of what the army did. It's easy to criticize if you weren't an adult back then or someone who didn't understand the politics that governed our thinking at that point in American history.

...We had not yet fully made the transition from a nation at war.

...There was Harry Truman still reeling from his sudden ascendancy to the presidency, toughened into steel by his decision to drop the atomic bomb on Japan and now faced with the monumental impact of a crash landing of a strange craft on American soil...."

From the Afterword—THE DAY AFTER ROSWELL
Col. Philip J. Corso, (Ret.) U.S. Army

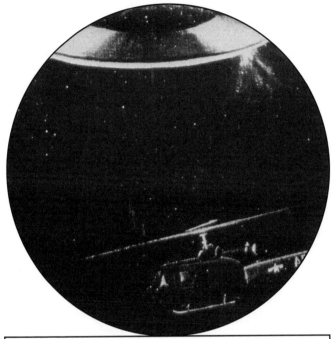

Lt. Colonel Lawrence J. Coyne and his crew encountered a big metallic-gray looking hull about 60 feet long.

CHAPTER 4
They Are Here!
Museum Exhibits—Glass Cases

A UFO is the reported sighting of an object or light seen in the sky or on land, whose appearance, trajectory, actions, motions, lights, and colors do not have a logical conventional or natural explanation, and which cannot be explained, not only by the original witness, but by scientists or technical experts who try to make a common sense identification after examining the evidence.

—J. Allen Hynek, The Center For UFO Studies

UFO Classifications

Classification System used by Center for UFO Studies founded by J. Allen Hynek

Close Sightings

CE1 Close Encounters (CE) of the First Kind
Though the witness observes a UFO nearby, there appears to be no interaction with either the witness or the environment.

CE2 Close Encounters of the Second Kind
These encounters include details of interaction between the UFO and the environment, which may vary from interference with car ignition systems and electronic gear to imprints or burns on the ground and physical effects on plants, animals and humans.

CE3 Close Encounters of the Third Kind
Occupants of a UFO—entities that are humanlike ("humanoid") or not humanlike have been reported. There is usually no direct contact or communication with the witness.

CE4 Close Encounters of the Fourth Kind
On board experiences or abductions of individuals, usually in the presence of humanoids. This classification was added recently, as reports of incidents involving very close contact even detainment of witnesses have increased.

CE5 Close Encounters of the Fifth Kind
Witnesses suffer physiological effects, permanent injuries, or death. (MUFON Field Investigators Manual)

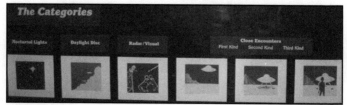

UFO Classifications

Distant Sightings

NL Nocturnal Lights
Sightings of well-defined lights in the night sky whose appearance and/or motion are not explainable in terms of conventional light sources. The light appears most often as red, blue, orange, or white. These form the largest group of UFO reports.

DD Daylight Discs
Daytime sightings are generally of oval or disk-shaped, metallic-appearing objects. They appear either high in the sky or close to the ground, and they are often reported to hover. They can seem to disappear with astounding speed.

See the book UNCONVENTIONAL FLYING OBJECTS by Paul Hill, former NASA engineer, for detailed information on these crafts' capabilities.

RV Radar Visual
Of special significance are unidentified "blips" on radar screens that coincide with and confirm simultaneous visual sightings by the same or other witnesses. These cases are infrequent.

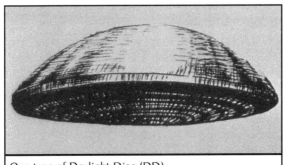

One type of Daylight Disc (DD).

UFO Sightings

Fifteen to Twenty Percent of UFO Reports Remain Unexplained
Modern UFO sightings are common now that we fly in
the skies with them, but many are not reported. Pilots,
astronauts and military radar personnel have reported
UFO sightings, but most have learned to keep quiet or
have been told to do so.

Photos, Lies and Videotapes

Early in this century, photography increased the aware-
ness of UFO activity. Hundreds of photographs of UFO's
display the variety—the many creative designs and colors
of these mysterious crafts. In the 1980s and 90s videotaped sightings have been shown on television worldwide.
Javier Maussan, a television producer in Mexico City,
requested UFO videos and received hundreds from his
Channel 7 viewers. A show including "the best videos of
UFOs" has been shown on television in the U.S.A.

Hoaxers have also made photos and videos of pie
pans and other contraptions and tried to pass them off
as flying saucers. Experts like Dr. Bruce Maccabee, however, have spent years perfecting the
analysis of these photos and videos
and still find many that are unex-
plainable.

Kenneth Arnold's sighting that
began the modern UFO era in June
1947 actually came after a long history of UFO activity. The difference was
that now the world had the technology to communicate quickly that UFOs
were seen and where.

CE2—The ground
under another spin-
ning dome sighting
showed evidence of
counterclockwise
movement.

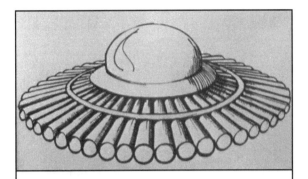

April 3, 1982
CE 2—Five witnesses reported sighting this object in two separate, but related sightings with evidence of changes in their yards and in their animals' behavior.

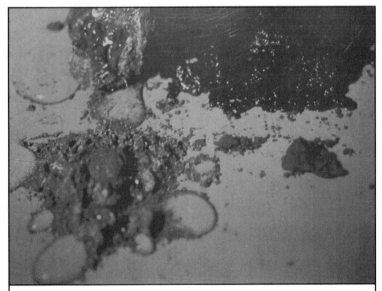

CE2 Evidence—Soil Test—Delphos, Kansas
In the photo directly above, droplets of water are rolling off soil (on the left) affected by a UFO. It won't absorb water. The normal soil (on the right) does absorb water.

Artist Unknown

Artistic interpretation of the Zamora sighting.

Police Officer Has Close Encounter

Socorro, New Mexico—April 24, 1964

While on duty, Patrolman Lonnie Zamora saw a car-sized object glowing with blinding light 800 feet from him. As he approached, he saw an elliptical shaped object. Then two short beings returned to their craft when Zamora got out of the patrol car to take a closer look. The object took off with a loud roar and then a whine. The object became silent for a short time before it disappeared from view.

Zamora called for backup and waited for State Trooper M.S. Chavez to arrive; then they examined the site. The elliptical object left burn marks on the ground. The short beings left footprints behind. All the physical evidence was photographed. Zamora now refuses to talk about his experience.

Recent Sightings

Some recent multiple sightings in the U.S.A. reported by MUFON in the *Mutual UFO Network UFO Journal* have occurred in Georgia, Minnesota, Iowa and North Carolina (Spencer 1997,1998).

MUFON also carried the Associated Press report of a UFO that nearly hit a Boeing 747 Swissair jetliner between Philadelphia and Boston enroute to Zurich, Switzerland on September 26, 1997.

Mutual UFO Network

MUFON has the only "UFO Information Center and Museum" in the U.S.A. east of Roswell, New Mexico. They are located in Seguin Texas.

Lunar Activity   Artist Joan Laurino
During the Apollo II mission, "Buzz" Aldrin and Michael Collins saw a cylinder that was really two connected rings. When they changed the focus on their sextant, the UFO looked like an open book (Marrs 1997).

For Those Who Want "Them" to Land on the White House Lawn

1952   UFOs "Buzzed" The White House

In June of 1952 there were 149 UFO reports. The Air Force became concerned. UFOs were sighted by employees at atomic installations all over the U.S. In July there were 536 UFO reports. UFOs were confirmed on radar over a period of several days in areas all around Washington D.C. On July 10, an airplane crew spotted a UFO over Quantico, VA. On July 13-14 more airline crews reported direct contact with UFOs that sped away at fantastic speeds near Washington. On the evening of July 20 three radar installations at Washington National Airport and Andrews Air Force Base showed targets three miles from the city. Then one appeared over the Andrew's radio tower. *The personnel went outside and witnessed a huge fiery-orange sphere. It hovered over them.*

On July 28 there were 58 reports in one day. The UFOs of that period were sighted by casual observers, radar operators, military personnel and were chased by Air Force jets. Twelve different objects had been spotted on radar. There were headlines all over the United States. At the press conference following these events the Air Force's position was: the radar sightings were the result of a temperature inversion. *Misinformation had become policy.* Temperature inversions are not seen as objects on radar and then seen moving away at fantastic speeds (Cousineau 1995); (Clark 1998).

Sightings Then and Now

Photographs are scrutinized, stories are rehashed and witnesses are badgered. In spite of those obstacles photographs remain, stories are passed on, and witnesses still have the courage to come forward.

Major UFO Areas in the World

For UFO Watchers

Africa—Central Africa, North Africa, around the Canary Islands

Asia —in Northern Japan, Central China and the Malaysian Peninsula

Australia—in the reef and rain forest region, Kempsey, Nullarbor region and Bass Straits

The British Isles—England, Scotland

Canada—Alberta (home of The Official UFO Landing Pad)

Europe—in Belgium, Spain, The Balearics and Provence, France; Pordenone, Italy

New Zealand and New Guinea

North America—Niagara, the Northwest states, Texas, New Mexico, Gulf area of Florida, Colorado, Michigan, Minnesota, Washington

Russia—Northern region

Scandinavia—Norway

South America— Argentina, Puerto Rico, Chile, Brazil (Randles 1992); (Cousineau 1995)

What are UFO Flaps?

Major waves of UFO sightings are normal. Year-long episodes are called flaps. Flaps have occurred all over the world in various year-periods. In fact, sightings have been recorded throughout human history; however, this chapter addresses modern sightings following the Kenneth Arnold sighting of 1947. Historical sightings will be discussed in later chapters.

The flap of 1947 was unique in the United States. Everyone was openly curious: the government, the Army Air Force and the media. People spoke their minds, their doubts, their skepticism. Those were the days.

> "Ridicule is not part of the scientific method and people should not be taught that it is."
>
> J. Allen Hynek

Following 1947, most people in the U.S.A. lost the freedom to openly discuss UFOs without fear of ridicule, loss of reputation, slander or death. In recent years, Shirley MacLaine, actress, shared her story of learning about UFOs and their occupants and one reporter said about her, "She doesn't have all her oars in the water." This is ridicule of sincere people looking for honest answers. When did this start?

Since 1947 there has been a consistent pattern of denial and misinformation given to the public. Was it because the army recovered the beings and saucers from New Mexico in 1947?

Gordon Cooper, Astronaut

Excerpt From a Letter to the United Nations 1978
"I believe that these extraterrestrial vehicles and their crews are visiting this planet from other planets, which are
obviously a little more advanced than we are here on Earth" (Marrs 1997)

Furnished by Barbara Lamb
Bythorn Mandala Crop Circle
1993

CHAPTER 5
Going Around in Circles
Museum Exhibit G
Crop Circles

Crop Circles

Sound like a good beginning to a farmer's love song? No, it's the name for the mysterious impressions and elaborate designs left in grass fields, particularly wheat, by an unknown force. Theories abound. How to explain:

- The grass sheath is not broken or burned.
- The grass sheath is bent and changed on a microscopic, cellular level.
- The grass that grows in that spot the following year may also be altered.
- Sometimes the grass strands are *braided together* or laid in a swirl pattern.
- They are made in the night.
- No person is seen through the night before they appear, despite repeated attempts at professional surveillance.
- The designs have become more elaborate over time. Now they may cover hundreds of yards.
- Thousands of crop circles have been identified all over the world.
- Their appearance has been associated with UFO sightings.
- People experience physical symptoms such as mental confusion and dizziness when standing in a true crop circle.
- Electronic equipment of various types, such as video cameras, quit functioning inside the circles.

Crop Circle Hoaxers Do Exist

Doug Bower and Dave Chorley, Englishmen from Southampton, confessed to making crop circles for fifteen years. So in 1991, in their 60s, they hung up their planks. Others have copied their stepping-on-a-plank method, but crop circle investigators have developed criteria to help winnow out the wheat from the chaff, so to speak. Even dowsers get into the act to determine the energy fields in a true crop circle.

What do Crop Circles Mean?

Crop circles suggest intelligence, an understanding of complex mathematics, a sense of design and beauty. The way the designs are made indicates harmlessness; the grass is not harmed, and attempts are made at communication; the symbols are getting more complex over time. It is as if we are being taught an alphabet. Symbols of any kind have a profound impact on our minds—these are extraordinary—and evoke the full range of human feelings of awe, fear and confusion.

They create speculation. Speculation takes us beyond the limits of our current beliefs and science to show us a vista of possibilities. Life is full of mysteries, the crop circles being one of the most beautiful.

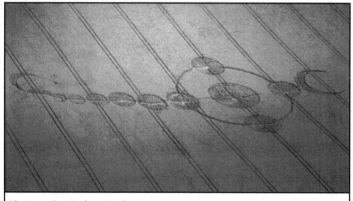

Photographer Barbara Lamb
Scorpion Crop Circle

Are Crop Circles Engineering Diagrams?

Human understanding of the crop circle "messages" may have made a giant leap forward in the 90s with the work of Doug Ruby. *He engineered propulsion systems and UFO-like spacecraft directly from the crop circle designs,* using them as engineering plans in a two dimensional code. *The Gift The Crop Circles Deciphered* by Ruby contains photographs of models designed from the crop circles. There are models of UFOs with each different type specifically demonstrating ascension, descent, angular and lateral motion.

Crop Circles—Are They Traffic Signs?

Another interesting hypothesis about the purpose of crop circles came from the remote viewers trained by the military. When the military ended their remote viewing program, some of the viewers established a private company. Remote viewing is a form of clairvoyance and consciousness bilocation such as an out-of-the-body experience where a target is seen psychically. There are strict scientific protocols that are followed so that results may be validated.

One of their experiments was to study the Barbury Castle crop circle with remote viewing. Remote viewers separately watched the same event and reported the same findings: a UFO-type sound and lights at the time the Barbury castle crop circle was formed.

In Jim Marrs' book, *Alien Agenda,* he reports the viewers received the idea that crop circles are like high tech traffic signs for aliens moving through both time and space. Crop circles need to be temporary to direct aliens through a specific time frame.

Doug Ruby, coincidentally, made a model of the Barbury Castle crop circle. From this most complex of all crop circles came a design for *a rotating beam gun.* This elegant piece of technology may play a role in the ascent of a UFO.

Force Fields May Propel the Crafts

Paul Hill, a NASA engineer, worked for 25 years on the engineering capabilities needed to propel UFOs. He took UFO witness' statements at face value and worked on the technical problems that needed to be overcome to achieve these maneuvers: the falling leaf or UFO rock, the silver-dollar

> *Army-trained remote viewers identified UFO sounds and lights while a crop circle formed.*

wobble, an acute angle turn, sudden reversal of direction, bank and turn, straight-away speed run and tilt to maneuver. He also examined their speed (up to 9,000 mph) and acceleration. Hill studied every aspect of the propulsion needed and the possible propulsive forces used. He concluded that force fields or acceleration fields were used to propel the craft. *Hill and Ruby essentially reached similar conclusions using completely different methods of investigation.* Hill states that every UFO maneuver falls within the realm of known physical laws. Ruby engineered these maneuvers using 2-dimensional diagrams to make 3-dimensional objects.

Photographer Barbara Lamb
Oliver's Castle Crop Circle

Crop Circles—Are they Music?

In the movie, *Close Encounters of the Third Kind,* the alien ship makes a tone for monks, for children and other witnesses. The UFO researcher, modeled after true-life UFO researcher Jacques Vallee, develops the tune that brings the UFO in and opens the magic door.

Are the crop circles a magic tune the aliens want us to learn? Could be....

The crop circle makers are elaborating on their designs over time. Doug Ruby found simple engineering designs preceded a complex engineering plan in crop circles. Researcher Freddy Silva explains that the precise geometry now found in many crop circles may be "notes" in parts of a scale. The notes are becoming more complex.

Cymatics research done by Dr. Hans Jeny showed a relationship between sound frequencies and shapes. He found that when a specific frequency is played through a membrane covered with a light substance, such as powder, symmetrical patterns can result. Some crop circles resemble sacred designs that have translated into certain chants to attain mystical states in Middle Eastern and Eastern cultures. Are there specific frequencies to be found within the complex designs? And if so, what do they "mean?" Is this a new language of sound?

> Sounds made as crop circles form have been analyzed by NASA's Jet Propulsion Laboratory.
>
> Their conclusions: Whatever is making crop circles is:
>
> 1. mechanical
> 2. vibrates at 5.2 kilohertz.
>
> —NASA

The Lid of the Tomb
of
Lord Pacal Votan
Is he seated in a spacecraft?

CHAPTER 6
Museum Exhibit G
Ancient Cultures and Their Connections to Extraterrestrial Life Forms

Tomb Lid of Pacal Votan

Pacal Votan: Extraterrestrial or an Extraordinary Mayan?
The design at the right was taken from Pacal Votan's
sarcophagus lid found by Alberto Ruz Lhullier in the
secret chamber of a Mayan pyramid located in The City of
the Serpents. This city is a stunning relic of an ancient
Central American culture whose people came with their
leader, Pacal Votan, from across the Atlantic some time
before 1000 BC. Their former home had been Tripoli in
Phoenicia. Votan may have been present at the Tower of
Babel. He described in writing about coming to a great
city, during his travels, where a temple was being built
to reach heaven, but was never completed because the
languages became confused. Some researchers speculate
Votan was an extraterrestrial.

The Temple of Inscriptions under which the tomb
was found had a hidden stairway covered by rubble. It
took four years to clear the rubble away—like mining for
a diamond—the tomb was buried underneath. Inside,
Lhullier found a six-foot tall white man. Mayans are typi-
cally five feet or so.

Erich Von Däniken interpreted the lid as a human
being bent forward in a spacecraft working the controls
with his hands and a pedal with his foot. Maurice
Chatelain sees the unmistakable image of a jet-propelled
craft.

If the lid were the only evidence of the unusual
advanced knowledge of the Mayans it might not be as
compelling. If, however, the discovery is put in the con-
text of the mathematical, astronomical and scientific
knowledge of the Mayans, the story of a culture led by an
astronaut concerned with astronomy and math makes
sense. As one small example, the Mayans calculated a
solar calendar that can predict an eclipse today within 13
seconds. They created phenomenal temples and observa-
tories. They had a far-reaching vision for their time
(Arvey 1989).

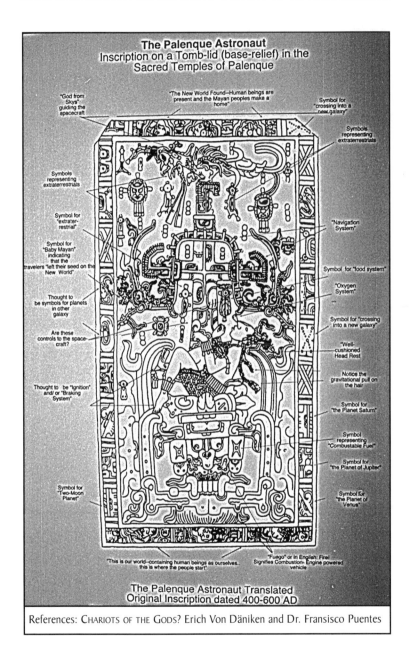

The Palenque Astronaut Translated
Original Inscription dated 400-600 AD

References: CHARIOTS OF THE GODS? Erich Von Däniken and Dr. Fransisco Puentes

Another Interpretation of the Tomb Lid of Pacal Votan

Maurice Cottrell, an engineer and independent scientist, thinks the lid tells a fascinating story, but not of space travel. In his book with Adrian Gilbert, *Mayan Prophecies*, he presents his translation of the story on the lid with beautiful color illustrations.

"In time these new stories were arranged into a second volume *The Amazing Lid of Palenque* Volume 2. Volume 2 was to contain the main 'spiritual 'message' of the Maya. It tells of the meaning of life and of the 'after life,' of purgatory and purification, and of the cycles of destruction on Earth.

"In the early days I had decoded the borders, but they had just been the 'index,' or list of contents, to a book. Then I had successfully decoded the book itself. But then the 'book' turned out to be just a programme (in the sense that when you visit the Theatre the 'programme' lists the actors and the plot). Finally I had come to realize that Volume 1 simply contained a list of the cast that appeared in Volume 2. Volume 2 was the 'performance' of the Maya. An incredible journey into the mind of man; an incredible journey of discovery. And, because of the layers involved in the structure and logic of the decoding mechanism, each of the actors appears up to six times in various costumes lending legitimacy to the decoding process. With such inbuilt redundancy there can be no ambiguity as to the intent of the Maya to transfer specific information."

By Maurice Cottrell, in *The Mayan Prophecies*, co-authored with Adrian G. Gilbert.

The Ancients Tell of Aerial Vehicles and Alien Beings With Special Powers

The Vedas

The oldest written texts in the world are the Vedas, which date back to at least 3000 BC. These writings are the Hindu religious scriptures. Flying machines, *vimanas*, are described in detail in many stories, as are the alien beings who pilot them. The information is strikingly similar to UFO and alien characteristics described today. The vehicles fly, glow, hover, appear and disappear. They have emanations that can harm people. The beings were classified by their characteristics. Diplomatic relationships were established with some of them. The beings had special powers, *siddhis*:

- Mental telepathy
- Hearing and sight over long distances
- Levitation
- Power to change the size of objects without disturbing their structure
- Telekinesis (moving solid objects with the mind)
- Ability to pass through solid objects
- Thought control at a distance
- Invisibility
- The power to assume various forms of being
- Possessing a human body

Richard Thompson, in his book *Alien Identities*, does a thorough comparison of current UFO sightings and past Vedic experiences.

> "One important point to make about ancient Vedic society is that aerial vehicles called vimanas in Sanskrit, were well known. They could be grossly physical machines, or they could be made of two other kinds of energy, which we call subtle energy and transcendental energy."
>
> Richard L. Thompson, ALIEN IDENTITIES

Who They Are—The Theories

Classifications
Humanoid-types: including genetically engineered cross-breeds
Animal-types: including the insect-like
Robot-type
Exotic (Huyghe 1996)

Humanoids
Grays— may have ancient, middle and advanced beings from their cultures visiting us all in the present as they are able to move through time as well as space.
Martians— a tall, thin race of beings that lost their home-world after a meteor struck their planet and destroyed their atmosphere. Live underground on Mars, the Moon and would like to "immigrate" to the Earth (Brown 1996).

Ancient Names That May Translate as Extraterrestrial
The Watchers—reportedly mated with humans
Nefilim-Sumer
Annunaki-Sumer
Devas-India (Humans may be descended from these)
Siddhas-India may correspond to the Sidhe-Celtic
Danavas-India may correspond to the Dana-Celtic
Rakshasas-India—the evil ones
The Elohim-Hebrew—the shining ones
Incubus-Roman—evil ones
Sucubus-Roman—sexual ones
Duses-named by the Gauls

Presumed Origins
The Pleiades
Reticulum
Mars
Earth's Moon
Moons of Jupiter
Other Dimensions

"Something is being seen, but it isn't known what... This formulation leaves the question of 'seeing' open. Something material could be seen, or something psychic could be seen. Both are realities, but of different kinds."
Carl G. Jung

How Long Have "They" Been Here?

Zecharia Sitchin, linguist, found UFO sightings were recorded in ancient documents. He can translate over 10 ancient languages. Piecing together the stories of the Sumerians, Babylonians, Egyptians, Mayans and others he has come to the conclusion that human beings have not only co-existed with extraterrestrials since their genesis, they were genetically engineered by those ancient astronauts.

The Sumerians kept careful records of UFO activity. Babylonians and Egyptians have many writings/drawings depicting flying craft. Cultures and tribes all over the world have passed down oral traditions of flying craft, gods, creators and floods. Sitchin puts this information all together and reveals new aspects of human history in his *Earth Chronicles* anthology.

Human Remnants Millions of Years Old

In Utah, William Meister found a footprint in shale that proved to be 505-590 million years old. Druet and Salfti found oval metal tubes of identical shape that were 65 million years old in France. Mrs. S. W. Culp found a finely crafted gold chain inside a piece of coal that was 260-320 million years old. In England, workmen uncovered a gold thread embedded in stone between 320-360 million years old. Other little known discoveries include: in Massachusetts, a silver, zinc vase with flowers beautifully inlaid with pure silver estimated to be over 600 million years old; in Oklahoma, an iron cup about 312 million years old; in Nevada, a shoe sole 213-248 million years old. The big mystery, however, is the grooved metallic spheres thought to be 2800 million (2.8 billion) years old found in South Africa. They are fibrous on the inside, covered by a type of metal that cannot be scratched with three grooves cut symmetrically into the base (Cremo and Thompson 1993,1996).

Imagine Finding This in Your Basement

In the basement of the Baghdad Museum in 1938, Dr. William Kong found a workable battery whose origins were dated to 2500 BC in Sumeria (Atlantis Rising Books 1996). This may support the Sumerian writings translated by Zecharia Sitchin describing extraterrestrials living right alongside Sumerians sharing their technology.

So Much for Darwin—Belief System Shock

The historians, archaeologists, biologists and paleontologists in the past have made theories based on the findings to their present day. Those, unfortunately, became our *beliefs*. When humans receive information or have an experience contradicting their beliefs they experience ontological shock—belief system shock—"What are my origins?" The most fundamental belief is the most frightening to lose. Millions of people on earth are now experiencing ontological shock as the technology of our age brings in a flood of new information.

Denial and anger are the most common reactions to the early stages of belief system shock. We all read about this in history when Europeans discovered the world was not flat. It was terrifying to them. Fortunately, advances in social science have provided many coping skills for this type of shock. This will be covered in Chapter 13, Coping with UFOs.

What Have "They" Been up to all this Time?

Judging from the mundane archaeological finds, "they" have been living a pretty ordinary life. They have relationships, sibling rivalry and wars according to the Sumerian, Hindu and Egyptian writings. We can only begin to understand the effect they have had on our understanding of history, sacred writings and miracles. Like older siblings, they pester, they tease, they hide, they teach and they have always been at least one step ahead of us —and this is a benign description of their activities, given our natural fearful reaction to them.

The Dark Side of Their Force

Some researchers are linking these beings to significantly more serious crimes against humanity, such as mass extermination on a periodic basis. Are "they" the brains behind *planned* epidemics like the Black Plague?

> "A great many people throughout Europe and other Plague-stricken regions of the world were reporting that outbreaks of the Plague were caused by foul-smelling 'mists'. Those mists frequently appeared after unusually bright lights in the sky. The historian quickly discovers that 'mists' and bright lights were reported far more frequently and in many more locations than were rodent infestations. The Plague years were, in fact, a period of heavy UFO activity."
>
> From William Bramley's, *The Gods of Eden* 1989, 1990

The Pattern of Extraterrestrial Governance

Bramley found a pattern of evidence that "they" use Machiavellian techniques to stir up hatred on both sides of a border to keep humans constantly at war with each other. He found this in political and religious conflicts.

The first human civilizations all over the globe shared similar odd governance laws. For example, if a ruler died the successor had to be a blood relative to the former ruler. If a ruler's wife died, the daughter would marry her father to keep the purity of the lineage. Brothers married sisters. This may have served to keep pure the genetically engineered qualities that the extraterrestrials desired of the human rulers. Another example of an odd similarity world-wide is the behind-the-scenes rule of government by secret societies since the beginning of civilization.

Jacques Vallee, through his research, concluded that "UFOs could well be part of the same larger intelligence which has shaped the tapestry of religion and mythology since the dawn of human consciousness (Vallee 1991)." He did not believe, however, that they directly governed humans in a traditional sense.

Other Ancient Artifacts

Many carved pieces, paintings, petroglyphs and heiroglyphs have images of halos or circles around heads of beings that may represent ancient records of extraterrestrial visits. Possible space helmets, energy radiations and electrical devices have been recognized in ancient artifacts the world over, now that the possibility of extraterrestrial visitation is more widely accepted.

A jet-propelled, one-seated spacecraft is now on display in the Istanbul Archaeological Museum in Turkey. Zecharia Sitchin worked with Museum officials to bring the artifact to the public display. Discovered in an ancient city, Tuspa, southeast of Lake Van, in 1975, the age of the artifact is as yet undetermined as is its authenticity, but the Urartu civilization is about two thousand years old. The spaceship is made of a porous, hard material like volcanic stone.

The Istanbul Museum believed it might have been a forgery because it does not reflect the style of the era nor were spaceships around at that time, so at first they didn't display it. Sitchin, however, was able to produce other carved images from that period similar to the artifact so the Museum put it in their exhibit collection.

Compare this one-manned space vehicle with that of the depiction on the tomb lid of Pacal Votan. This piece may be 1000 years older than the tomb lid, and yet there are some striking similarities. Both people have bare feet. The vehicles' noses end at the same approximate place on the pilot's bodies and tail pipes jet out the rear.

Istanbul Archaeological Museum   Artist C.P. Leacock
Spaceship Artifact with Pilot's Head Broken From Carving
600-800 B.C.

Retrofit (Bas-relief)
Donor & Artist
Bob Turner

CHAPTER 7
"You Won't Believe What I Saw"
Museum Exhibits H & I
Personal Experiences

Patrolman Herbert Schirmer

On Dec. 3, 1967, Patrolman Schirmer had an instinct that something was amiss as he drove through Ashland, Nebraska. He saw what he thought was a broken down truck at the junction of two highways and got out to investigate. He saw a flying saucer take off. When he got back to his car to write his report he was missing half an hour. He had a bad headache and a bruise down his neck.

Under hypnosis he was able to recall being on board the craft with small beings. They told him their purpose was to prepare people for their existence.

Artist—Joan Laurino

Schirmer, an Army brat, did not expect this outcome. He didn't believe in flying saucers, but he was so affected by the event he quit the police force.

The Gulf Breeze Sightings

Ed Walters' perseverance in photographing UFOs in Gulf Breeze, Florida, provided the world with solid evidence of the crafts. Working with the Mutual UFO Network and Dr. Bruce Maccabee, Walters and his wife, Frances, took hundreds of photos with a stereo camera, a regular 35-mm camera and a

Artist—Joan Laurino

Polaroid™. He also videotaped footage of the awe-inspiring UFOs.

In *The Gulf Breeze Sightings*, the Walters' tell the detailed story of the early sightings in 1987 and then close encounters of the third kind through 1988. Ed began to recall missing time earlier in his life. Then he was abducted at the end of the UFO photography project. Budd Hopkins began to work with Ed to remember and deal with his abduction experiences.

William J. Herrmann

Herrmann experienced numerous abductions from Nov. 1977 through 1983. A mechanic in Charleston, NC, he found himself among small men about 4-5' tall with gray-white skin and very pronounced large eyes. The men wore one piece suits fitted at the neck. The suits had no insignias or fasteners of any kind. They told Herrmann they were from the constellation Reticulum. Herrmann refused a polygraph test.

Artist—Joan Laurino

COMMUNION and FIRE IN THE SKY
Whitley Strieber and Travis Walton

Nearly 200,000 abductee and visitor experiencers have written Whitley Strieber since the publication of *Communion* in 1987. Some of these letters are reprinted in *The Communion Letters* by Strieber and his wife, Anne. As the Striebers point out in this book, there is concrete evidence not only of abduction, but that *implantation is occurring* as abductees such as Ed Walters in Gulf Breeze, Florida have claimed.

Dr. Roger Lier tested implants recovered from abductees at the National Institute for Discovery Sciences at New Mexico Tech. Beings with technologically-advanced science created these implants. Sophisticated knowledge was used to make them. They are made with either minerals to resist rejection by the abductees or body membranes made from the abductees skin (Strieber and Strieber 1997).

Why do aliens abduct humans, put implants in their bodies and conduct medical experiments on them? Abductees have been told various things by the aliens, including: their species needs help with reproduction; the

abductee is actually "one of them" in temporary human form; they are creating the next species of humans; or, they are trying to spare us from planetary self-destruction. Investigators have put forth other theories: this level of trauma implants deeply in the mind so that abductees will recall their abductions; abductees are being programmed by the "new myth" aliens are trying to create in human culture; or, that aliens are slowly conditioning us to their presence. No single answer has emerged.

The abduction experiencers give us insight into the capacities of the alien beings. Abductees describe aliens' abilities similarly, despite the differing appearances of the beings. They are telepathic and clairvoyant. They have the ability to "know" each of the abductees to the core of their being—to the point of awe and discomfort. Aliens move through 3-dimensional objects and can levitate humans and move them through walls.

They either have the technology or the mental power to temporarily paralyze humans. Some aliens reportedly lack human emotion and empathy, and therefore do not treat humans with dignity and respect for their personal boundaries. Some abductees describe meaningful and ongoing relationships with certain aliens. There seems to be as wide a variety of human-alien relationships as there are human-human relationships.

Travis Walton's abduction in 1975 and Whitley Strieber's life-long abductions by aliens are the most well-known. Walton has written two books about his experiences, *Fire in the Sky* and *The Walton Experience*. Strieber has written many books about his experiences: *Communion, Transformation, Breakthrough* and *The Secret School* and a "fiction" book about the Roswell incident, *Majestic*. Each author has had a film made of their abduction experiences, Walton's *Fire in the Sky* and Strieber's *Communion*. They are available on videotape.

The Betty and Barney Hill abduction in 1961 was the first widely publicized abduction. Their story was written by John G. Fuller in *The Interrupted Journey*.

Excerpts of their story appeared in national magazines in the 1960s.

Abductees have turned the most terrifying experiences ever described by human beings into carefully documented accounts, so that others may benefit. As Kathy Mitchell stated in *Abducted!*, she is not trying to prove aliens exist, she is trying to cope with her experiences (Jordan and Mitchell 1994). Walton, Strieber and others have all suffered tremendously— not only in the abductions, but possibly even more so from the collective human reactions to their experiences. There are many others who have come forward with the courage to tell their stories, despite threats to their personal credibility.

John S. Carpenter MSW/LCSW has worked with nearly 100 clients recovering from the effects of UFO encounters. In making a psychological assessment, he states the symptoms of the clients are consistent with Post Traumatic Stress Disorder caused by an external stress perceived as real by the experiencer. His clients have had good coping skills, but needed therapeutic support for the trauma (Haley 1993). Researchers are making advances in the treatment of trauma. A promising therapy is Eye Movement Desensitization and Reprogramming (EMDR), found to very successful in treating Viet Nam war veterans, disaster victims and other trauma survivors.

It Took Courage

Without the testimony of the courageous abductees, none of this information would be available. Evidently these stories have struck a chord in many other people. Many of these stories have been tested by law enforcement lie detectors. Most notably, in Travis Walton's case, six men witnessed his abduction and passed voluntary lie detector tests *while he was still missing.* Walton later passed a lie detector test after he was returned by the aliens. You could lay odds of a million to one that these seven corroborated stories are true (Walton 1978,1996).

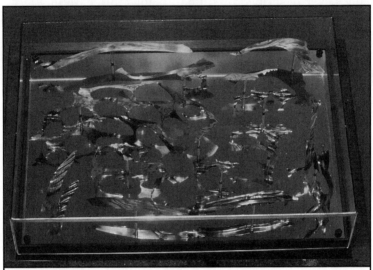

Photographer Miller Johnson

The "wood grain metal" scraps in this display case are from jeweler Randy Fullbright's Utah shop. Case and contents donated by Miller Johnson.

CHAPTER 8
Museum Exhibit K
Roswell: The 1996
Metal Fragment
Incident

"Smuggled Debris"

In March 1996, a Roswell citizen gave a piece of debris he claimed came from the 1947 Roswell crash site to the Museum. The IUFOMRC's dedication to research opened a door for the analysis of this piece that otherwise might have remained closed. Initially, Max Littell, a museum officer, arranged for an x-ray fluorescence analysis at the New Mexico Bureau of Mines and Mineral Resources. The 1.616 gram fragment of "debris" contained a combination of copper and silver, with traces of sodium, aluminum, silicon, iron, chromium, sulfur and chlorine. Miller Johnson, Research Director for IUFOMRC contacted Larry Callis of Los Alamos National Laboratory (LANL) and began negotiations to have further analysis that would identify the fragment's origin as earthly or extraterrestrial. The museum's unquestionable desire for scientific evidence of the fragment's origin led the way for LANL to take the piece for study.

Miller Johnson and his wife, Marilyn, spent two days at LANL to oversee the project as the scientists did their analysis. John Bass from LANL Media Relations recorded the analysis for the museum at Johnson's request. Larry Callis and his team used a Thermal Ionization Mass Spectrometer, one normally used for analysis of nuclear materials. The spectrometer found the isotopic ratios measured on two fragments were typical of terrestrial values. They came from earth.

One unusual attribute of the fragments still remained a puzzle: the layering of the metals. Fragment #2 had eight alternating layers of silver and copper in its .001 inch thickness. Fragment #1, however, had 19 layers of silver and copper in a .0133 inch thickness.

For Johnson, the mystery was 99% solved when Randy Fullbright, a jeweler in St. George, UT identified Fragment #1 as a scrap from his studio. Johnson's research also concluded Fragment #2 to be a positive match with another scrap from Fullbright's studio. Case closed.

VISITOR
INFORMATION

The Lobby of the IUFOMRC

Please sign our guest register and put a push pin on the
map (to your left) to show where you are from.
You can come back to the lobby to sit and relax in a
comfortable chair at any time during your visit.

The International UFO Museum and Research Center received the Top Tourist Destination for New Mexico from the Governor in 1997.

CHAPTER 9
Visitor Information
We Welcome You!

MUSEUM INFORMATION

The International UFO Museum and Research Center
114 N. Main St.
P.O. Box 2221
Roswell, New Mexico 88202
Phone: 1-800-822-3545
        (505)625-9495
FAX: (505)625-1907
email: iufomrc@lookingglass.net
web site: www.iufomrc.com
Monthly Publication: *The IUFOMRC Newsletter*

Location: On the west side of Main St. between 1st and
2nd streets.

Hours: Labor Day to Memorial Day :10 A.M. - 5 P.M.
       7 days a week
       Summer Hours from
       Memorial Day to Labor Day: 9 A.M.— 5 P.M.
       7 days a week
       Open all holidays except closed on Thanksgiving
       and Christmas
       Admission: Free
       Donations accepted

Children: Children are Welcome
        Children's Play Area Provided.
        Please do not leave children unattended.
        See also —Children's UFO Chapter 11—They can
        read it themselves.

Museum Tour Tape

by Bob Barnes

This professional production of narration for each exhibit includes sound effects and eerie music to accompany your visit. Pick up the cassette and tape player with head set at the desk.

The Video Rooms

Two Video Rooms
Videos about Roswell and UFOs play continuously during museum hours. Ordinarily, there is no video schedule and it is likely you can view a particular video you are interested in. Check with a volunteer for a list of titles.
Video Room #1
This spacious room is located adjacent to the Roswell Timeline Exhibit with two entrances, one at the front and one at the back of the room.
Video Room #2
This room is located to the left of the auditorium area.

Rest rooms

Rest rooms are located at the back of the Museum at each corner—Women on the right and Men on the left.

Alien Caffeine Espresso Bar

Relax and enjoy a snack in the midst of posters of your favorite science fiction movie characters. A wide variety of snacks are available.

The Gift Shop & T-Shirt Heaven

Visitors love our souvenirs and t-shirts. We also offer a wide variety of books and tapes on UFOs and extraterrestrials.

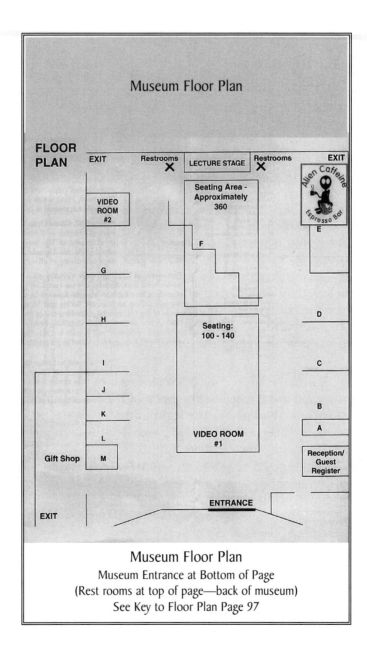

Museum Floor Plan

Museum Entrance at Bottom of Page
(Rest rooms at top of page—back of museum)
See Key to Floor Plan Page 97

MUSEUM EXHIBITS—Key to page 96

Exhibit A
Alien Examination — See Chapter 1

Exhibit B
Roswell Incident Timeline — See Chapter 2

Exhibit C
Roswell Incident Timeline Part II — See Chapter 2

Exhibit D
Mogul Balloon Display — See Chapter 3
Roswell Case Closed by the Air Force
Anthropomorphic Crash Dummy

Section E
ALIEN CAFFEINE ESPRESSO BAR

Section F
Auditorium Area

Exhibit G
Crop Circles — See Chapter 5
Ancient Civilizations and ETs — See Chapter 6

Exhibit H & I
Poetry, Personal Experiences,
Photographs and Diagrams of UFOs—See Chapter 7

Exhibit J
Our Universe — not included in guidebook

Exhibit K
The 1996 Metal Fragment Incident — Chapter 8

Exhibit L
Humor and UFOs

Section M — Tour Information Office

IUFOMRC'S Membership Program

By becoming a member IUFOMRC, you connect yourself with the clearinghouse of information relating to UFOs and the phenomenon surrounding the entire subject. You will receive a monthly edition of *The IUFOMRC Newsletter.*

With the IUFOMRC a major advocate for the Freedom of Information Act, you will receive the bare, unadulterated truth of events happening around the world in relation to the UFO phenomenon. Every Member is extended an invitation to all programs scheduled within our Museum.

Membership Types & Benefits

General Membership—$25/year
- Official Membership Card
- Monthly Museum Newsletter
- 10% discount on all Gift Shop purchases
  (mail orders also)

Sustaining Membership—$50/year
- All benefits of General Membership
- 15% discount on all Gift Shop purchases

Participating Membership—$100/year
- All benefits of Sustaining membership
- Official Museum Mug

Sponsorship/Commercial Membership—$250/year
- All benefits of Participating Membership
  (Limited to four membership cards/mugs)
- Check-out privileges of Library materials
- These funds are used to provide UFO books to
  elementary schools nationwide

Lifetime Membership—$1000 One-time donation
- All privileges of above described memberships

We also offer a Gift Membership Club. Looking for that hard-to-find gift for the person who has everything? Sign them up as a member, including the first year's membership fee. With the New Member's Packet, the recipient will receive an official Museum mug and a personalized card for the occasion. Please include the giver's complete mailing address. Let us take care of your gift giving.
We are a 501(c)(3) non-profit organization—all of your donations and membership fees are completely tax-deductible.

IUFOMRC Mission Statement

The International UFO Museum & Research Center was organized to inform the public about what has come to be known as "The 1947 Roswell Incident." The Museum collects and preserves materials and information in written, audio and visual formats that are relevant to the 1947 Roswell Incident and other unexplained phenomena related to UFO research. The Museum endeavors to be the leading information source in history, science and research about UFO events worldwide.

The International UFO Museum's constituents are committed to gathering and disbursing to all interested parties, the most qualified and accurate up-to-date information available. We make this our responsibility, as we feel the more information you have, the better you will understand this phenomenon and the more informed your decisions will be. Any contributions of information, personal experiences, artifacts or research material pertinent to our matters that can be made available to this museum are greatly appreciated by all—especially the public we serve.

Whether taking your stance as an American citizen under "The United States Freedom of Information Act," or as a citizen of any nation, by standing together with us the whole truth will be known.

Our Commitment

The IUFOMRC, a non-profit organization located in Roswell, New Mexico, is dedicated to providing information regarding the Roswell Incident of 1947, and related information concerning UFO and Extraterrestrial phenomena.

We welcome every visitor and pledge to assist you. Any contributions of information, personal experiences, or research materials are greatly appreciated.

Together, we can arrive at the truth; together the truth can be known. With a growing library of archival materials valued over $250,000, and programs to provide UFO books for schools nationwide, education is the primary goal of the Museum.

Visitors From 1992—1997 Three Hundred Thousand	
1992	1,494
1993	11,743
1994	29,445
1995	33,300
1996	69,015
1997	192,124
	337,121 Total Visitors

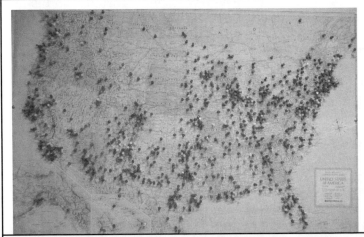

Map 3   Visitors come from all over the world. Many visitors, 24,583 to be exact, came from the U.S.A. the first week in July 1997—the 50th year anniversary of the Roswell crash.

Beauty and Fear

Artist—Dan Garmus

Museum Exhibit UFO Art Gallery

Art and Writing

The Museum is proud to be an artistic center, as well as information center, for display of paintings, weavings, sculptures, carvings, photographs, and poetry and other arts related to the UFO phenomena. Paintings can be purchased at the museum.

Since the beginning of history, art has been a means of coping with events as well as recording them. Unique beings, gods, creatures and flying craft have all

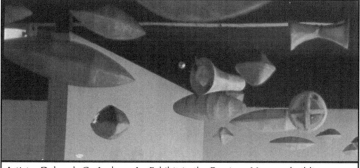

Artist—Deborah G. Aschen An Exhibit in the Previous Museum building

Donor and Creator —Ashley Waterfall Company
Alien Waterfall

been the subject of works of art in various forms.
From the pictographs of the ancients to the plays of the
Greeks, people have sought to deal with beings with
super-human attributes. In the Greek play, *The Birds* by
Aristophanes (448-380 BC) humans are attempting to
overthrow the rulership of the gods. The birds of the sky
are to be the mediators. Why? The humans are sick of
taxes imposed by the "gods." (And we thought the IRS
was tough.) Reading the ancient plays while imagining
the gods to be ancient astronauts puts a whole new light
on why we might think of them as classic stories that
have meaning in our lives.

There are so many intelligent forms that have
appeared to people: flying dragons; flying mothmen;
thunderbirds; the dog-headed Anubis. And the witnesses

Artist—Markus Tracy
We Have Five of Them

have faithfully recorded the shapes. Now you can see the head of a grey alien on guitar straps, key chains and television commercials. One thing is certain! These extraterrestrials are imaginative in the forms they take.

Today, many of us are using art as a way to express our feelings about UFOs—the fear and awe of viewing a higher intelligence and the vastness of the physical universe.

Artist—Von Tipton
Old Barns and Alien Objects

The Roswell Incident Mural
How It Was Created

Designer/artist Miller Johnson created this original full-color art with ink and markers on a small sketch pad. He then photographed his illustration as required by Computer Image Systems. They used a revolutionary process to transfer the crash site photo image onto fabric for an 8x12 foot mural. The photo image was read by a laser scanner which separated the colors and digitized the information onto a permanent tape. This tape relayed color information to four electronic airbrushes loaded with the colors magenta, cyan, yellow and black. These colors were sprayed in precise amounts onto the mural fabric from the four airbrushes in a consecutive 2mm width line until the mural was completed in 35 minutes. The mural was then stretch-mounted on a wood frame.

Highlights of the Museum's History

It Began In 1992

Newspapers around the U.S. carried the 1992 story: a UFO Museum would open in Roswell, the site of the 1947 Roswell Incident. Walter Haut and Glenn Dennis had been on the scene during those fateful days in July 1947. Wanting to preserve the memories, their intent was to establish something the

The International UFO Museum and Research Center made national news from the beginning.

community would be proud of and to draw people to Roswell to do research. At that time the Chamber of Commerce was receiving several thousand inquiries about the incident each year.

January 1992

The first Museum building opened on the seventh floor of the Sunwest Center in January 1992 with a membership program that included 100 members who had donated $100 each. Max Littell organized the business of the museum.

October 24, 1992

The Museum moved to 406 N. Main St.; 38,000 visitors from around the world had come since its opening.

The 10,000th visitor Maiko Hipple, one and a half years old, stands with her parents John and Mary Hipple and her baby sister.

In 1993

RALF - The wooden alien statue sculpted by Oregon artist, Steiner Karlsen 1993, donated by Bruce Meland, publisher of *Electrifying Times*, Bend, Oregon. RALF was named by Teresa Douglas from Amarillo, TX, in the Name the Alien Contest.

September 1994

The movie *Roswell* was filmed in the summer of 1993. It was unusual in that it was not a science fiction story, but rather a human military drama about the RAAF base and surrounding community. *Showtime Network, Inc.* aired it in September of 1994. Executive producer, Paul Davids, is a UFO witness. Prior to the making of the film he spotted one near Pasadena, California.

January 16, 1994

The Washington Post printed an article about the Roswell incident after U.S. Representative Steve Schiff called for an investigation into the 1947 event. His request did not mention UFOs. He wanted to know about the documents concerning the incident. He received a terse reply from the Air Force stating he needed to look in the National Archives, but the Archives claimed they didn't have any documents either.

January 1995
Stan Crosby, Roswell UFO Encounter Committee chair-
man, was responsible for the first annual Roswell UFO
Festival. He prepared the city for the international
attention it received during the celebration of the 50th
anniversary.

June 16, 1996
Museum presents replica of Mayan tomb inscription—
Hand-carved by Dr. Francisco Puentes of El Paso, TX,
this wood replica 9'x9' true-to-scale replica of the lid of
the tomb of Lord Pacal, a ruler of the Mayan empire
which is thought to have existed between 400-600 AD.
    The tomb was discovered in 1949 by Alberto Ruz
Lhullier in a hidden underground passage. A well-pre-
served white man was found in the tomb. This Mayan
was 70 inches—taller than the average Mayan at 60
inches. The lid depicts a possible astronaut sitting at the
controls of a space vehicle.

December 1996
The museum received the Top Tourist Destination 1997
by the Tourism Association of New Mexico in December
1996 at the Governor's conference on tourism.

January 1, 1997
The Museum opened its doors in the present location,
114 North Main St., with close to 500 active members,
and a IUFOMRC Kids Club.

July 4, 1997
Roswell Encounter
The Museum received national media attention again.
This time over 300 news media reporters and television
cameramen came during the Roswell UFO Encounter '97
the 50th Anniversary of the Roswell Incident.

July 18, 1997
Kent Hawthorne of Champaign, Illinois, was the
250,000th visitor to the Museum.

February 1998
Library Expands Ten-fold
Expansion of the Museum library occurred with new
donations of over 30 bookcases of books and new files.
One collection was valued at over $250,000.

Hall-Poorbaugh Press presents Aliens
and UFOs —an art competition for
young people. Ryan Calkins won the grand
prize with the drawing of an alien face.

Downtown Roswell outside the IUFOMRC on a quiet summer evening. The horizon can be seen in all directions. Blue sky is abundant.

CHAPTER 10
Roswell, New Mexico
History
Tourist Attractions

Roswell —What is it Like?

The anticipation of seeing Roswell can be intense. What is a place like where a flying saucer has crashed? The strip into town is USA all the way—McDonald's, Denny's, Holiday Inn. Closer to downtown the buildings are older and the businesses privately owned and long held. The hardware store near the museum focuses strictly on hardware with a display window touting various sized galvanized tubs. A mountain range stands at a distance over an otherwise completely open horizon.

The IUFOMRC resides in the Old Plains Theater building in the center of downtown. Free parking adjacent to the museum is a welcome surprise. Ordinary experience stops at the entrance; nothing prepares you for a first tour through the museum. No matter how many television shows, movies, books or newspaper and magazine articles state the fact of UFO observation, being in a gallery of experiencers and their stories is profound. The IUFOMRC is the main attraction to tourists coming into Roswell. There is a lot more to Roswell, however.

Roswell and Chaves County

Roswell is proud to have the largest bus manufacturing plant in the world, also the largest mozzarella plant. Christmas ornaments are also manufactured here. Chaves County, in which Roswell resides, is primarily an agriculture—business oriented community producing wool, alfalfa, chili, cotton, pecans and livestock.

The land in the county is inexpensive with abundant water and utilities to support ranching, farming and the dairy industry.

The people of Roswell and the surrounding area have a reputation for hospitality, diversity and a pioneering spirit.

Roswell—Other Attractions

Roswell Museum and Art Center, 100 W. Eleventh St.,
Hours: Monday —Saturday, 9:00 A.M.-5:00 P.M.; Sundays
and Holidays, 1:00 P.M. -5:00 P.M. *Free Admission.* The
Aston Gallery of Bronzes is a special feature.
(505)624-6744.

Robert H. Goddard Planetarium, located at the Roswell
Museum and Art Center, includes the Robert H. Goddard
Workshop Replica, 100 W. Eleventh St.
Public shows one week per month, Tuesday through
Saturday 1:30 P.M. and Friday evenings, 7:30 P.M.
General Admission $2; Museum members $1. Laser Light
Shows $5. (505)624-6744.

Roswell Convention & Civic Center, 912 N. Main St.
North entrance to view mosaic mural. Hours: 8:00 A.M.-
5 P.M. Monday through Friday.

Historical Center for Southeast New Mexico, 200 N. Lea
Ave. Open Friday, Saturday, Sunday 1 P.M.-4 P.M. Special
tours by appointment. Closed all holidays.
 Admission: Adults $2, Children under 12, free.
(505)622-8333

General Douglas L. McBride Museum (New Mexico
Military Institute) 101 W. College Blvd. Hours: Tuesday-
Friday 8:30 -11:30 A.M. and 1:00 - 3:00 P.M. Closed all
holidays. *Free Admission.* Educational programs by
appointment. (505)624-8220

More Roswell Attractions

Anderson Museum of Contemporary Art, 409 E. College Blvd. Hours: 9:00-12:00 P.M. and 1:00-4:00 P.M.

Spring River Park and Zoo, 1306 E. College. Hours: 10:00 A.M.-8:00 P.M., 7 days a week. *Free Admission.*

Goddard Rocket Museum, 100 W. Eleventh St., at the Art Museum. Same hours. *Free Admission.*

Spring River Hike & Bike Trail, Spring River Park, 1011 W. Fourth St., (parking available), 5.5 miles of paved scenic hike and bike trail. (505)624-6270.

Bitter Lakes National Wildlife Refuge, Office hours: 7:30 A.M. to 4:00 P.M. Best viewing times are 1/2 hour before sunrise and 1/2 hour after sunset. (505)622-6755

Bottomless Lakes State Park, Swimming, hiking and fishing. For information call (505)624-6058.

Roswell—The Five Day Tour

Highlights
IUFOMRC
Ragsdale Crash Site
Corona Debris Field
Corn Ranch Crash Site
Ruidoso, NM
Alamagordo, NM
Carlsbad Carverns

For information call
SAI Tour Office
IUFOMRC
505-625-9495 or
505-623-8104

HI!
I am RALF, your guide to the UFO Museum. Welcome! I hope you learn some new things and think about them. Can you find me in the museum?

CHAPTER 11
Children's UFO Chapter*

*Third Grade Reading Level

What is a UFO? Do you know the *initials* for your first, middle and last name? The first letter of each of your three names are your *initials*. U F O are *initials* for the name Unidentified Flying Object.

People cannot always name the flying objects that they see in the sky. Any object we don't know in the sky is called unidentified. Have you seen something you didn't recognize flying in the sky? Some people see helicopters, planes or satellites so far away they can't tell what is flying. Sometimes people see things close but don't know what they saw. It could be an Air Force test plane. And sometimes people see objects that fly that no person on earth seems to know anything about. Some people think that these objects are spacecraft that come from other planets.

Do you know where this picture is in the museum? Hint: it's in a picture with a helicopter in a glass case.

Many people think there are no spacecraft from other planets and all these objects must come from earth. Other people think that these objects come from an invisible place called another dimension. That is the mystery in the UFO Museum. What do your parents, brothers or sisters think?

Do you like to solve mysteries? While you are walking through the museum, you will see

photographs, paintings and drawings of UFOs.
Can you guess what these funny-looking
objects are and where they come from? Not
even your friends or family know for sure. So
your guess is as important as anyone else's.
When you grow up you might find out your
guess is right!

So, UFOs might be spacecraft from other
planets. They might be something else. The
grownups do not agree whether spacecraft have
come to earth from other planets. Isn't it
strange not to know something this important
for sure?

I am an alien, or
some people call
me an E.T.

What
is an alien?

The name alien means
somebody who doesn't live here.
When we talk about space aliens
we mean somebody who doesn't
originally come from earth. You may have seen
the movie, *E.T.* the letters E. and T. are initials
for extraterrestrial. That's another name for
aliens: E.T.s and extraterrestrials. You may also
hear them called beings, creatures or grays.
Can you think of other names for aliens?

Did you see the naked dummy at the front
of the museum? He is a pretend alien some
people made for a movie called *Roswell.* He is
naked because in the movie the doctor did an
autopsy. An autopsy is an operation to find out
why someone died. In the movie, this alien died
in a UFO crash.

Many people have seen aliens and told other people their stories. They also wrote their stories down and drew pictures of meeting aliens. Movie studios have made movies about the aliens people have seen and UFOs that have crashed. In the UFO Museum you will see some of these.

Some of the paintings and drawings are

just pretend aliens and spacecraft. Can you pick out a picture that you think is pretend? The artist didn't really see an alien like the one in the painting, he made it up. Can you make up a picture and a story about an alien when you get home?

The above painting done by Srapnal Zoie is a pretend picture. I think it's scary. Do you?

Some people think that all stories and pictures about aliens are made up. Isn't that confusing? Just like UFOs, not everyone agrees that aliens have come to earth. What do you think?

If you think you have seen an alien, or if you see one in the future, it is very important that you tell a grownup you trust. Some people

t sad, mad and scared when they
eet an alien. Do you think you
ould? Most people get scared when
ey see someone that looks different
r the first time. Have you seen
abies cry when they sit on the lap of
meone they don't know? They are
ared by someone who looks different.
is natural and normal to be scared of
meone we don't know.

id a UFO with aliens in it crash in oswell, New Mexico?

Many people in Roswell remember
ashes in three different places more
an 50 years ago. A UFO may have
xploded over one place, Foster ranch,
ıd crashed in another, the Pine Lodge
ea. Or two saucers may have hit each
her, with one crashing near Pine
ɔdge and one near the San Agustin
lains. The pieces of metal and plastic
at a few men saw didn't look like

The first time I ever saw humans, I was very scared. You are big and have fuzz all over your heads. And the hairy arches above your eyes scared me. What do you call those things?

ıything made on earth. Some other men and a woman
w a crashed UFO. There were little aliens who died in
ıe crash in a place nearby. And at San Agustin plains
ı New Mexico, a family, a teacher, his students and
nother man saw a two dead aliens, a dying alien—*but
ıey also saw a live one.* He had tried to help the other
liens; there was something like a first aid kit nearby.
he alien didn't talk to them. People heard the alien's
ıoughts in their minds. He died later at the hospital.

The Army came and took the pieces away to show

scientists so they could find out what crashed. Some men from the Army said a weather balloon crashed, other Army men said a spacecraft with aliens on board crashed. We do not know who has the pieces or the bodies now.

In 1994 the Air Force wrote a report saying the balloon that crashed was a Mogul Balloon. It doesn't look like a regular balloon. It was huge, like a hot air balloon, with testing pieces like three radar targets hanging 650 feet down. The Mogul Balloon

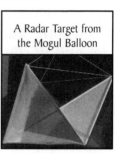

A Radar Target from the Mogul Balloon

was testing for nuclear explosions in Russia, so the Army didn't tell anyone about it. It was Top Secret. They also say in their report that the bodies people found were crash dummies. A

Harold

Crash Dummy named Harold is displayed at the back of the Museum by the Alien Cafe. Did you see Harold?

If it was a flying saucer, why would the Army and Air Force tell a different story?
If spacecraft from another planet did crash then, it was right after World War II. The Army men may have been worried. Many people were attacked during the war and they were afraid aliens might attack the earth. The Army men may have decided to protect

everyone on earth from the truth so no one would be scared. Maybe they were scared too, and didn't know what to do.

The Army told the people in Roswell who saw the pieces of the metal and plastic to keep it a secret. And the people did what the Army men told them. Everybody kept the secret. Finally one man from the Army, Colonel Jesse Marcel, who had picked up the pieces and put them in his car in 1947, thought the people on earth should know that he thought a flying saucer had crashed. *He told the secret*, but many years after it happened. Then other people felt safe to tell the secret: Colonel Corso, Steve Mackensie and Major Easley. Sergeant Thomas Gonzales even told about the Army finding five little alien bodies.

When people started to tell the secret, many American people didn't believe them. The secret had been kept for so long that even if it was true, people said they were making it up.

Colonel Marcel didn't work for the Army anymore so he couldn't get back the pieces he had found to prove he saw a flying saucer. Then it was hard to prove that a spacecraft crashed because the Army and Air Force did not show anyone the pieces that the people found. The people in the Army, Air Force and United States government still say there is nothing that shows a saucer crashed in Roswell; but they may need to keep it a secret if the crash is TOP SECRET. It is their rules. It is hard to be sure if they are telling the truth, if the crash is secret.

Museum Visitors—Lauren and Shannon Elward
Corona Impact Point
DONOR—G.W. Dodson

Kid's Favorite Exhibits

Alien Examination of the dummy made for the
Showtime Original movie *Roswell*.
The I-beam near the photo of Jesse Marcel Jr.,
MD, in the red shirt; He was 11 years-old when

his army dad told him a flying saucer crashed near Roswell. See the violet symbols on a piece of the crashed disk; maybe aliens like *violet writing.*

Did you ever write with a purple marker?

Pieces of Debris made to look like the crashed spacecraft pieces based on descriptions from people who saw the real pieces. The parts could not be torn, cut or burned. The metal was light as a feather. When it was wadded up and dropped on a table it went back to its original flat look.

The Radio Station Room where the story of the crashed spacecraft started to go out to all the people in the world. The government stopped it. This is what a radio station looked like in Roswell in 1947.

Through the Eyes of the Children
The Wall of Kid's Drawings is located on the far left of the Auditorium Hall, next to the stage.

RALF standing next to the beautiful **mural.**

Ancient Drawings—Some look like children's drawings of aliens from the past. Aliens from other planets may have always visited earth.

Paintings by Artists
Pictures of how artists view planets, spacecraft, aliens and places on earth that aliens may have been.

Drawings by People Who Have Seen Aliens
What people remember happened to them when

they thought they met aliens and saw space-craft from another planet.

Photographs of UFOs
Are these spacecraft from another planet?
Large Black and White Diagram of UFOs reported to the Congress of the United States are the different shapes of UFOs people have reported.
Posters of Outer Space are pictures and photos of planets and the solar system.
Mystery Metal —Did it come from the Crashed Flying Saucer at Roswell? Probably not. This metal turned out to be from earth, made by an artist in the U.S.A.
Make a souvenir of the Museum from a penny. Watch the machine flatten it like a pancake.

Bye!
Thank you for coming. Come and visit me again and bring your friends. I would like to meet them!

The Gift Shop has toys and books, especially small alien figures and spacecraft, to play out all the stories in your imagination. Small things to remember your important visit.
AND T-shirt Heaven!

All men by nature desire
knowledge.
    —Aristotle

CHAPTER 12
Belief, Theory, Evidence and Proof

What Proves that Something Exists?

So, George, How Many Did You See?

On September 1, 1997 the Associated Press announced that physicists *discovered* an elusive subatomic particle, a meson. Fifty-one physicists involved in the experiment *didn't actually see the exotic meson*: they deduced its presence! [Author's emphasis] So it is now discovered and accepted.

Over time, hundreds of thousands, probably millions, of people have witnessed UFOs, including at least "51 scientists," and still the scientific community and the established press do not announce the discovery of UFOs or admit their existence. Nor do other governments in the world.

For those who say there is no scientific evidence, no solid, concrete evidence of UFOs: they are mistaken or they have changed the rules of what constitutes evidence. Some people believe we have enough evidence to have proof of UFOs.

The Difference between Belief, Theory, Evidence, Proof

Belief is what makes sense to you. It's your convictions based on what you've heard and what you've trusted to be true about reality. It has been proven to you.

Theory is what makes sense to you that also makes sense to others. There is evidence, but no proof.

Evidence is made up of pieces of information, testimony and objects that *tend* to prove something, but do not actually prove it.

Proof is a collection of information, testimony or objects that define a reality. In mathematics there is a defined way to arrive at a proof. In science the amount of evidence needed for proof of something is less defined. (You can see the problem with that just in all the changes in opinion that take place in medical research.) In criminal

law, proof is what evidence it takes to convince a jury, usually 12 people, that a person is guilty. In civil law, it may take only one judge.

Interestingly, in UFOlogy there never seems to be enough evidence to prove the existence of UFOs or extraterrestrials. Since there is no defined amount of evidence needed to prove the existence of UFOs, some scientist or government official can always claim there is not enough evidence for *proof.* So it becomes an individual decision. How much evidence does it take to prove that UFOs exist, for you?

What Is the Evidence that UFOs Exist

The IUFOMRC is a collection of evidence that UFOs exist. This evidence includes the photographs and videos that have been scientifically proven to be genuine; the testimony of witnesses to UFOs and extraterrestrials that has been scientifically proven through polygraph; the physical evidence of crop circles scientifically found to be made by a machine with a defined vibration.

There is proof that stems of wheat, barley and rye have been changed microscopically after a UFO has been seen hovering over or landing on them. Dirt has been proven through chemical analysis and observation to have been altered in composition, caused by a UFO as seen by witnesses. Burns on witnesses of UFOs have been medically proven to be radiation burns. Radiation burns are hard to come by unless you are getting radiation therapy.

Colonel Philip Corso was a witness to reverse-engineering the technology we obtained from the Roswell saucer: lasers, kevlar vests, fiber optics, silicon chips and night-vision goggles. No one has come forward to claim they invented this technology from scratch.

Author David Morehouse was a participant in the remote viewing scientific studies done by a special army unit from the 70s to the 90s. He encountered extraterrestrials, in the special unit. Remote viewing is done under strict scientific protocols.

You will find witness affidavits in the exhibits, more testimony from witnesses in the stories on the

walls, and voices of the witnesses describing their encounters on the tour tape. Many more close encounter witness testimonies can be found in the book section of the gift shop.

Now You May Say, "I'm Convinced. There Is Proof that UFOs Exist— But it Doesn't Feel Good."

If you are one of our visitors, who is considering the evidence and think it is adequate proof of UFOs and extraterrestrials, you will begin a process of coping with that information. Most people experience some symptoms of belief-system shock (ontological shock). The coping skills found in the next chapter, developed by others who have faced this same turning point, may help you.

Our understanding of ourselves and our place in the universe changes as we reexamine historical documents with the possibility of extraterrestrial capabilities in mind. We can imagine their capabilities more easily than anyone in history because of our own technological advancement. When historians in the past came across "tales of gods with magical powers," there was no *Star Trek* presenting the possibility of technological powers. Those historians had no concept of these advancements. Therefore, they interpreted the translation of ancient writing with what they knew to be possible. What is possible is changing daily in our highly technological society.

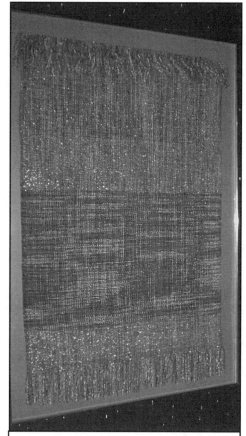

Weaver—Bella Sue Martin

UFOs appeared in this weaving unplanned.

CHAPTER 13
Coping with UFOs
Changing Beliefs

Individual Coping

Denial is the first coping mechanism every human uses. Denial is the necessary tool of the mind to protect our complex mental and emotional natures. Even those people with first-hand experience of UFOs and aliens go in and out of denial. For example, what do we say when a good thing happens: "I can't believe it." And what do we say when a bad thing happens: "I can't believe it." The mind handles trauma by alternating thoughts of "it happened" with "it didn't happen" to allow the deeper aspects of the mind time to process the event. Trauma overwhelms us biologically and physically. It affects our central nervous system. Sometimes when our belief systems change we experience trauma.

Telling others about our new experiences or new UFO information is usually the next step in coping. Many of us stop here in processing new UFO information or an experience. Many people have encountered painful opposition to their experiences and have learned to keep quiet.

Now there are people in various organizations and professions helping others to cope with new UFO and alien information and experiences. The IUFOMRC is one of those organizations. The volunteers at the Museum answer thousands of questions and hear many UFO and alien experiences.

The next coping stage people move through is expressing their feelings verbally, in writing, and through the arts. You see much evidence of this in your visit to the IUFOMRC. While the evidence of experiencers is available at the Museum, to validate what you have heard, you are encouraged to come to your own conclusions. There is space available in the IUFOMRC members' monthly newsletter for your written theory about the phenomena. You can submit your art: stories, poems, paintings and artifacts to the Museum. (Not all of them can be displayed of course, but there is a place for them.)

HOW TO COPE with UFOs and Aliens

•Denial protects the mind. Respect your denial.

•Identify what you are feeling about the existence of UFOs/aliens.

•Write the feelings down: e.g. excited, awed, angry, scared.

•Use the arts to express your feelings: Paint~Write~Sculpt~Dance.

•Look for hints of UFO alien experiences in the arts of others: e.g. the paintings of Dali. He may represent aliens as ants and there are alien shapes in many of his paintings. The feelings of being abducted come across in melting clocks, et cetera.

•Read the writing of other experiencers and their professional counselors (see References).

•Read the myths of ancient cultures.

•Write down your dreams and work with them.

•Watch a video e.g. *X-Files, Fire in the Sky, Roswell, Communion, Independence Day, Men In Black.*

•Laugh—Use humor in every possible way
  Example: One abductee put different color cartoon-character bandages on each of her toes just to "blow the aliens' minds!" (Collings and Jamerson 1996).

•Join or create a discussion group.

These typical coping skills are not intended to be substituted for professional help when you are not coping or have experienced trauma.

Cultural Coping

One could interpret various cultural histories as having recorded and coped with UFOs and extraterrestrials in unique ways. The ancient Greeks wrote and watched plays about the Gods that acted out their frustrations and fears.

Cyclops by Euripides specifically deals with the chaos that one hybrid—a child of earth and heaven as he refers to him—creates through his savagery. *Medea*, another play by Euripides, deals with a female hybrid who has mental powers—Euripides refers to her as a sorceress; she kills humans, including her own children, with no regrets.

These plays have remained important to literature for 2500 years. You may not have appreciated them while you were in school and had no interest in the "mythology" of the Greeks. Read the myths and plays now and you will find an outpouring of the anger the Greeks felt at the control the gods had over their lives.

Many ancient cultures, as we see in the IUFOMRC, used pictorial representations of the ceremony of the "gods." Some wrote scriptural records of these interactions with the "gods." Music was written to please them. Animal sacrifices were made to them. Food was offered to them. Poetry was composed for them. All to cope.

The Vedic cultures have been the most advanced in history in their diplomatic relations, trade and communication with various types of extraterrestrials. They defined the "good" guys and the "bad" guys and described their appearance, their vehicles and their actions.

The Vedic people of the Indian subcontinent also had members of their culture whose job it was to remain in altered states of consciousness to maintain telepathic connection with all types of extraterrestrials.

To this day, yogis and other mystics dedicate their lives to maintaining these states of consciousness, although their encounters are misunderstood by many in the West. Not having clearly defined categories of these beings, many Western practices lump all these beings into a "sacred" category.

The Tibetans are more clear in their teachings to Westerners that there are demons in other realms. Buddha described attacks by these demons as he sat, determined to attain the highest state of consciousness.

Most religions have a tradition of dealings with some type of evil, non-human higher intelligences. Most also have a belief in a higher intelligence of pure love and goodness with emissaries to spread this message. These beliefs are kept apart from scientific belief and there hasn't been a bridge.

In free countries, individuals have had the freedom to develop their own beliefs and there will be a huge variety in how people will cope with changing these. Proof of UFOs will challenge everyone in some way: religious, scientific, political or personal (safety, psychic boundaries).

All this is to say that collectively we are going through an enormous revolution in our thinking, but are doing it by inches, by ourselves, with little support. Our cultures are coping unconsciously with these changes.

In the 20th century we wrote books, took photographs and produced television shows and movies. The arts have always been a fine outlet for human fear and frustration. Think of the popularity and, therefore, the cultural importance of *Independence Day*, the movie "everyone" went to see. We cope with what we know about UFOs as a culture unconsciously because it is not the norm to discuss them openly. Great possibilities are ahead as we legitimize UFO and extraterrestrial research. The universe is probably a far more magnificent place than we presently imagine.

GLOSSARY
REFERENCES
ACKNOWLEDGEMENTS
INDEX

Glossary

AF— United States Air Force

alien (abb. for space alien)—a being not originating from Earth

Army Air Force (U.S.)—the U.S. Army and the U.S. Air Force were a combined military service until 1947 when they separated into different services.

anthropomorphic crash dummies—human-like bodies manufactured to test the safety of equipment used by humans. Specifically, the dummies used by the U.S. Air Force in parachute tests that the AF now claims were the bodies found in the desert by the Roswell Incident witnesses.

CE—close encounter; used as part of a classification system to describe the details of the encounter

extraterrestrial—a being not originating from earth, synonymous with space alien

flap—a time period over which there are frequent sightings of UFOs

Foo fighter—balls of light seen by the Allies and enemy World War II fighter pilots, often during dog fights

I-beam—a piece of the flying saucer debris found near Roswell in 1947; it had violet hieroglyphs on it.

IUFOMRC—The International UFO Museum, located in Roswell, New Mexico, U.S.A.

Majestic-12 (MJ-12)—The team of 12 men appointed by President Harry Truman to analyze the UFO and alien presence discovered in the USA in 1947.

Mogul Balloon—a code name for a U.S. Army Air Forces program to detect and monitor Soviet nuclear weapon tests.

polygraph test—lie detector test administered by a professional

RAAF—Roswell Army Air Force Base, home of the 509th Bombardment Group, the men trained to drop the atomic bombs

reverse-engineer—an engineering process of taking an existing piece of equipment without an available design and creating the design to manufacture the piece of equipment. Used specifically when foreign technical equipment or alien technical equipment is designed from an existing piece of recovered material.

teletype machine—a communication device used before fax machines to transmit words onto paper

UFO—unidentified flying object; more recently—unconventional flying object

References

Andrews, George C. 1993. *Extraterrestrial Friends and Foes.*
Illuminet Press, P.O. Box 2808, Lilbum, GA 30226.
ISBN: 0-9626534-8-9. $14.95.
   This overview of the extraterrestrial phenomena covers a
broad range of research and speculation. Controversial conspir-
acy theories include linking the assassinations of our leaders in
the 1960s with an extraterrestrial agenda. Encourages a greater
understanding of the types of groups—benevolent and malevo-
lent—that may be visiting earth.

Arvey, Michael. 1989. *UFOs: opposing viewpoints.* Greenhaven
Press, Inc., P.O. Box 289009, San Diego, CA 92198-9009.
ISBN: 0-899080-6-0X.
   The evidence of UFOs and aliens spawned a great deal of
speculation. This fine work gives many viewpoints on the differ-
ent theories about the phenomena.

Atlantis Rising Books Editors. 1996. *The Search for Lost Origins.*
Atlantis Rising Books, P.O. Box 441, Livingston, MT 59047.
ISBN: 0-9653310-0-8.$14.95.
   An anthology of articles from a hot new magazine, *Atlantis
Rising.* Interviews and articles by the researchers of earth's for-
gotten past: Zecharia Sitchin, Graham Hancock, John Anthony

West. Information on current scientific discoveries of earth's energy fields and ancient information that unlocks today's questions.

Berliner, Don and Stanton T. Friedman.1992,1997. *Crash at Corona: The U.S. Military Retrieval and Cover-up of a UFO.* Marlowe & Company, 623 Broadway, New York, NY 10012. ISBN: 1-56924-863-X. (Paperback) $13.95.
    This is an objective, carefully analyzed report of the Roswell Incident with many specific quotes and detailed explanations. Original researcher and interviewer Stanton Friedman has a solid basis of experience with Roswell witnesses.

Berlitz, Charles & William L. Moore. 1980. *The Roswell Incident.* Berkley Publishing Group, 200 Madison Ave., New York, NY 10016. ISBN: 0-425-12602-1. $5.50.
    One of the first major works on the Roswell crash and the coverup. Contains a chronological table of astronaut UFO sightings from 1963-1972.

Bramley, William. 1989,1990. *The Gods of Eden.* Dahlin Family Press: The Hearst Corporation, Avon Books, 1350 Avenue of the Americas, New York, NY 10019. 1993. ISBN: 0-380-71807-3. $5.99.
    As an historian, William Bramley sought the causes of war in world history. Every thread led to some UFO involvement. He quit the project again and again. His findings of extraterrestrial involvement were ridiculous, he thought. Eventually, he wrote a book. Well researched with interesting theories.

Brown, Courtney. 1996. *Cosmic Voyage.* Onyx. Dutton Signet: Penguin Books USA Inc., 375 Hudson St., New York, NY 10014. ISBN: 0-525-94098-7. (Hardcover) $23.45. ISBN: 0-451-19026-2. (Paperback) $6.99.
    A personal quest by a remote viewer to answer multiple questions about extraterrestrials, specifically the Gray species and the Martian species. Trained by an army-trained remote viewer, Brown sought answers to the questions we'd all like answered in double—blind sessions of remote viewing with scientific protocols. The answers he received were reassuring and challenging. A controversial work.

Clark, Jerome. 1998. *The UFO Book: Encyclopedia of the Extraterrestrial.* Visible Ink, 835 Penobscot Bldg., Detroit, MI 48226-4094. ISBN: 1-57859-029-9. $19.95.

Clark, the former editor of the magazine for the J. Allen Hynek Center for UFO Studies has done a great service to UFO researchers and the public alike by producing a complete two-volume, *The UFO Encyclopedia. The UFO Book* is an abridged volume of that work. It contains the major cases and modern historical overview in just 705 pgs. A perfect reference for anyone wanting to see the evidence of UFOs, as well as those who are researching specific questions.

Collings, Beth & Anna Jamerson.1996. *Connections: Solving our Alien Abduction Mystery.* Wildflower Press, P.O. Box 726, Newberg, OR. 97132. ISBN: 0-926524-35-6. $17.95.

These courageous women first presented their stories at the MIT Abduction Symposium 1992. This chronicle of repeated abductions and their efforts to cope is invaluable for any abductee. Gives others a compassionate look into the daily struggle abductees experience.

Corso, Colonel Philip J. (Ret.) 1997. *The Day After Roswell.* Simon & Schuster, Inc: Pocket Books, 1230 Avenue of the Americas, New York, NY 10020. ISBN:0-671-00461-1. $24.00.

The first published account verifying the Army's possession of the Roswell craft and the extraterrestrial occupants. The author not only witnessed the remains right after the crash, he was also in charge of disseminating the technology from the spacecraft through Research and Development at the Pentagon. This created the biggest technological explosion in the history of mankind: silicon chips, lasers, fiber optics, kevlar vests, and much more.

Cousineau, Phil. 1995. *UFOs: A Manual for the Millennium.* HarperCollins Publishers: HarperCollins West 10 East 53rd St., New York, NY 10022. ISBN: 0-06-258638-6. (Paperback) $5.99.

An excellent value for all the information packed between the covers. Lots of interesting trivia alongside graphics, charts and an overview of the UFO phenomena.

Cremo, Michael A. and Richard L. Thompson. 1993. *Forbidden Archeology: The Hidden History of the Human Race.* Bhaktivedanta Book Publishing, Inc., 3764 Watseka Ave., Los Angeles, CA 90034. First Edition, revised, 1996. ISBN: 0-89213-294-9. $44.95.

This book is a collection of archeological finds that established archeological circles have not integrated into their worldview because the evidence doesn't fit current theories of evolution and the standard timetable. Highly respected archeologists lost reputations when trying to bring this new evidence to light. Includes evidence of man-made objects millions of years old.

Dennis, Glenn. 1991. *1947 Roswell Incident.* IUFOMRC Gift Shop. Pamphlet. $7.50.

This eyewitness account by a highly respected New Mexico Funeral Director (now retired) brings the Roswell Incident home. This account is as straight forward as its author. This is pivotal information available to the public of what happened in 1947.

Downing, Barry. 1968,1997. *The Bible and Flying Saucers.* Marlowe and Company, 632 Broadway, New York, NY 10012. ISBN: 1-56924-745-5. $13.95.

The Bible is a sacred, unquestionable book for many people in the world. Downing makes a respectful approach to examining some evidence of extraterrestrial involvement in the lives of Biblical religious leaders and their people.

Fowler, Raymond E. 1981. *Casebook of a UFO Investigator.* Prentice-Hall Inc, Englewood Cliffs, NJ. 07632. ISBN 0-13-117432-0 (Hardcover); ISBN 0-13-117424-X (Paperback).

Details on UFOs abound from the 50s and 60s, those sometimes glossed over by current investigators and authors . Good historical reference. Significant similarity in past and present sightings and experiences.

Friedman, Stanton T. 1996,1997. *Top Secret/Majic.* Marlowe and Company, 632 Broadway, Seventh Floor, New York, NY 10012. ISBN: 156924-830-3 (Hardcover); ISBN: 1-56924-741-2 (Paperback) $13.95.

A thorough and convincing evaluation of the authenticity of documents regarding the existence of the secret Presidential advisory group Operation Majestic-12.

——— 1997. The Roswell Story, *MUFON 1997 INTERNATIONAL UFO SYMPOSIUM Proceedings*, Mutual UFO Network, Inc., 103 Oldtowne Rd., Seguin, TX 78155-4099. 196-205. $25.00

A serious review of the facts of the Roswell Incident clarifies many mistaken notions put forward by the media. Specific information.

Gilbert, Adrian and Maurice Cotterell. 1995. *The Mayan Prophecies*. Element Books, Inc., P.O. Box 830, Rockport, MA 01966. ISBN: 1-85230-692-0. $24.95.
Years of research went into this detailed reference of discoveries in the Mayan civilization. The analysis of the meaning of the Lid of the Tomb of Pacal Votan does not support the alien astronaut theory. Rather it gives a glyph by glyph interpretation consistent with other Mayan writing interpretations. An important work to bring objectivity to the search for evidence of alien influence on earlier civilizations.

Haley, Leah H. 1993. *Lost Was the Key*. Greenleaf Publications, P.O. Box 8152, Murfreesboro, TN 37133. ISBN: 1-883729-03-3.
Another good abductee reference from a female point of view. The author tells how her understanding has evolved about the forces behind the extraterrestrials and how she has coped. Its a good example of how someone has worked through denial.

Hill, Paul R. 1995. *Unconventional Flying Objects: A scientific analysis*. Hampton Roads Publishing Company, Inc., 134 Burgess Lane, Charlottesville, VA 22902. ISBN: 1-57174-027-9. (Paperback) $15.95.
For 25 years, Paul Hill worked full time for NASA and part-time on his theories about the engineering feats of UFOs. He was the unofficial NASA collector of UFO documentation. His work details the capabilities of UFOs and the engineering necessary for their characteristic patterns. Readers without an engineering background can understand the material presented in layman terms.

Hopkins, Budd. 1981. *Missing Time*. Ballantine Books, 201 E. 50th St., New York, NY 10022. 1988,1989. ISBN-0-345-35335-8.
A classic reader of abduction histories by a well respected, caring UFO researcher and founder of the Intruder's Foundation. Captivating details keep it lively.

Huyghe, Patrick. 1996. *The Field Guide to Extraterrestrials*. The Hearst Corporation: Avon Books, , 1350 Avenue of the Americas, New York, NY 10019. ISBN: 0-380-78128-X. $12.50.
This one-of-a-kind ET watchers guide contains over fifty illustrations of the various lifeforms taken from eyewitness accounts associated with UFO sightings. Not suggested for bedtime reading.

Hynek, J. Allen and Jacques Vallee.1975. *The Edge of Reality.*
Henry Regnery Company, 180 N. Michigan Ave., Chicago, IL
60601. ISBN: 0-8092-8209-7 (Hardcover). ISBN: 0-8092-8150-3
(Paperback).
   The culmination of these two brilliant men's years of
research; this discussion outlines their theories of UFOs and
the origin of the beings who operate them.

Keel, John A. 1991. *The Mothman Prophecies.* IllumiNet Press,
P.O. Box 2808, Lilburn, Georgia 30226. ISBN: 0-9626534-3-
8.$16.95.
   Rich in details surrounding the famous Point Pleasant,
West Virginia UFO flap of 1966-67. A broad-minded approach to
the underlying phenomena that manifest as UFOs, concomitant
paranormal phenomena, and Men in Black. A good read.

Jacobs, David Michael. 1975. *The UFO Controversy in America.*
Indiana University Press, 601 N. Morton St., Bloomington, IN
47404.
   An academic's approach to research of the UFO phenomena and the Condon report; it's thoroughly enjoyable. Rich in
detail from the period of the 1960s and 70s and an overview
that includes the history of sightings since the 1800s. Good reference.

Jordan, Debbie and Kathy Mitchell. 1994. *Abducted! The Story
of Intruders Continues.* Carroll and Graf Publishers, Inc., 260
Fifth Ave., New York, NY 10001. ISBN: 0-7867-0129-3. $21.00.
   These sisters have done a remarkable job of revealing the
inner experiences of an abductee family. The story was originally reported by Budd Hopkins, a dedicated abductee advocate, in
his book, *Intruders: The Incredible Visitations at Copely Woods.*
Now Jordan and Mitchell are ready to come forward using their
real names to share the growth they have experienced.

Littell, Max, Editor.1996. *Roswell: The "Naked" Truth about the
1947 UFO Crash at Roswell.* Ragsdale Productions, Inc. P.O.
Box 1881, Roswell, NM 88202. $14.95.
   Jim Ragsdale and his girlfriend may have been the only
eyewitnesses to the actual crash of the flying saucer in 1947.
This account, researched under the guidance of the
International UFO Museum and Research Center, is a fascinating report that pulls together more evidence of the Roswell incident and the aftermath.

McAndrew, Captain James. 1997. *The Roswell Report: Case Closed.* The United States Air Force, Superintendent of Documents, U.S. Government Printing Office, Washington, D.C. $18.00.
    This young author does a remarkable job of pulling together the evidence, the Army Air Force activities and events that went on before and after the Roswell Incident of 1947 and trying to make it fit some of the witnesses' statements. Omissions of critical witnesses' testimony and speculation that crash dummies dropped several years after 1947 were mistaken for aliens dented its credibility. Photographs and maps make a nice military historical document.

Marrs, Jim. 1997. *Alien Agenda: Investigating the Extraterrestrial Presence Among Us.* HarperCollins Publishers, 10 East 53rd St. New York, NY 10022. ISBN: 0-06-018642-9. $24.00.
    Written by an extraordinary journalist, this book is a good read if you only read one on alien theories. Contains the most interesting speculations and information in the 20th century.

Morehouse, David. 1996. *Psychic Warrior.* St. Martin's Press, 175 Fifth Ave., New York, NY 10010. ISBN: 0-312-14708-2. (Hardcover) $23.95. ISBN: 0-312-96413-7. (Paperback) $6.99
    A must read. Absolutely. Scientifically acquired evidence by the United States Army remote viewing team that extraterrestrials exist. Morehouse "paid" for the publication of this book with the loss of his army career and benefits. Answers to some of life's mysteries.

Preston, Richard. 1997. *The Cobra Event.* Random House, 201 E. 50th St.,New York, NY 10022. ISBN: 0-679-45714-3. (Hardcover) $25.95.
    A page-turner fiction about bio-terrorism. Preston's research of government agencies and bioweapons flies by with a fast-paced story.

Randle, Kevin D. USAF, Ret. 1989. *The UFO Casebook.* Warner Books, Inc., 666 Fifth Ave., New York, NY 10103. ISBN: 0-446-35715-4.
    A fine collection of UFO lore including more on Kenneth Arnold and his sighting at Maury Island. Also the Tunguska explosion in Russia and Minnesota mutilations. Covers

sightings and government response from 1947—1988.

———— and Donald R. Schmitt. 1991. *UFO Crash at Roswell.* The Hearst Corporation: Avon Books, , 1350 Avenue of the Americas, New York, NY 10019. ISBN: 0-380-76196-3. $5.99.
These two researchers have compiled more eyewitness testimony to the Roswell Incident than anyone.
————. 1994. *The Truth About the UFO Crash at Roswell* ISBN: 0-380-77803-3, $6.99.
An up-to-date compilation of the Roswell Incident events with hundreds of excerpts from personal interviews.

Randles, Jenny.1992. *UFOs and How to See Them.* Sterling Publishing Company, 387 Park Ave. S., New York, NY 10016. ISBN: 0-8069-02973-3.
A comprehensive guide to UFO hot spots by a world reknown authority. An interesting manual full of valuable information for UFO seekers.
———— and Peter Hough. 1994. *The Complete Book of UFOs.* ISBN: 0-88069-8132-0. $14.95.
This volume focuses on international sightings of UFOs, abductions and animal mutilations. This is a highly reputable source book. Good background for understanding the similarities of UFO activities worldwide.

Ruby, Doug. 1995,1997. *The Gift: The Crop Circles Deciphered.* Blue Note Publications; Blue Note Books, 110 Polk Ave., Suite 3, Cape Canaveral, FL 32920. ISBN: 1-878398-14-8. $32.95.
Ruby's ideas are revolutionary. There is nothing to compare with the work he has done to build models from the crop circle designs. No scientific or engineering background is necessary to enjoy his finely illustrated work.

Saler, Benson, Charles A. Ziegler, and Charles B. Moore. 1997. *UFO Crash at Roswell: The Genesis of a Modern Myth.* Smithsonian Press, Washington D.C. 20560.
ISBN: 1-56098-751-0. $22.45 Hardcover.
Examines how a myth is created in this prestigious volume. Unfortunately, the underlying presumption the reader may make is that the Roswell Incident must not have involved extraterrestrials and their craft, since myth implies a fictitious story. Although some Jungian scholars admit the possibility that myths originate from events in another dimension, most readers are unfamiliar with that interpretation.

Silva, Freddy. 1998. Music in the Fields: Is There a Sound Explanation for the Crop Circle Phenomenon? *Atlantis Rising Magazine*, No. 14, 42-42, 70-71. Editor, J. Douglas Kenyon, P.O. Box 441, Livingston, MT 59047.
Background on the various research that brings mathematical, vibrational and musical evidence to bear on possible interpretations of the crop circles.

Sitchin, Zecharia. 1985. *The Wars of Gods and Men: The Third Book of the Earth Chronicles.* The Hearst Corporation: Avon Books, 1350 Avenue of the Americas, New York, NY 10019. ISBN: 0-380-89585-4. $5.99.
Answers many questions about the Egyptian "gods" and their true identities. Connections are made to the Sumerian Annunaki (people from space). Who built the pyramids and why. Densely packed with research.

———— 1990. *Genesis Revisited: Is Modern Science Catching Up with Ancient Knowledge?* ISBN: 0-380-76159-9. $5.99.
This is a good introductory book for those who are just beginning to read Sitchin's work. A good overview of his translation of Sumerian texts and the space travel, genetic engineering and human colonization by the ancient extraterrestrials.

Shawcross, Tim. 1997. *The Roswell File.* Motorbooks International Publishers & Wholesalers, 729 Prospect Ave., Osceola, WI 54020. ISBN: 0-7603-0471-8. $24.95
This volume not only includes an overview of the Roswell Incident, but an analysis of the film of the alleged *Alien Autopsy.* Also has up-to-date information on documents supporting the Roswell Incident.

Spencer, John, Editor. 1991. *The UFO Encyclopedia.* The Hearst Corporation: Avon Books, 1350 Avenue of the Americas, New York, NY 10019. ISBN: 0-380-76887-9. $15.00.
This reference is a must for anyone reading about UFOs internationally. Written by a British author and director of the British UFO Research Association, this material is comprehensive.

Strieber, Whitley. 1987. *Communion: A True Story.* The Hearst Corporation: Avon Books, 1350 Avenue of the Americas, New York, NY, 10019. ISBN: 0-380-70388-2. (Paperback) $5.95.
One of the most famous abduction stories ever written.

The first in a series of books about the author's life-long relationship with the "visitors". Vulnerable, frightened beyond imagining, this man faces those he thinks are demonic and begins to transform.

Strieber, Whitley and Anne Strieber, Editors. 1997. *The Communion Letters*. HarperCollins Publishers; Harper Prism, 10 East 53rd St., New York, N.Y. 10022-5299.
ISBN: 0-060105368-6. $13.00 (Paperback).
Of the nearly 200,000 letters the Striebers received from people sharing their experiences of the "visitors" and UFOs, the authors chose a cross section of examples of various types of experiences. An immediate taste of the vast phenomena some people are experiencing with few places to share it.

Spencer, David T. 1997. Current Cases. *MUFON UFO NETWORK UFO JOURNAL*. Mutual UFO Network, Inc., 103 Oldtowne Rd. Seguin, TX 78155-4099. October 1997. 8-10.
The journal of a most highly respected international UFO organization. Contains frequent Roswell evidence analysis, book reviews, debate on the latest theories and new sightings and evidence.
———— November 1997 16-18.
———— December 1997 11-13.
———— January 1998 12-14.
———— March 1998 14-17.
———— April 1998 20.

Thompson, Keith. 1991. *Angels & Aliens: UFOs and the Mythic Imagination*. Ballantine Books: Fawcett Columbine.
ISBN: 0-449-90837-2. $12.00.
A Jungian-myth approach to the interpretations of UFO sightings. Based on the theories of psychologist, Carl G. Jung, this work gives the reader latitude to explore the psychological dimension of the UFO experience.

Thompson, Richard. 1993,1994. *Alien Identities: Ancient Insights into Modern UFO Phenomena*. Govardhan Hill, Inc., P.O. Box 52, Badger, CA 93603. ISBN: 0-9635309-1-7. 1995. $19.95.
A comprehensive explanation of the significant similarities between ancient Hindu sightings and present day sightings.

Tiedemann, Arthur E., Editor. 1974. *An Introduction to Japanese Civilization*. D.C. Heath and Company.

ISBN: 0-231-03651-5 (Hardcover); ISBN- 0-669-52878-1(Pbk).
Chapters on early Japan describes "the UFO pattern" of creation, deities, religions, brother-sister marriage among the deities, government design and the spreading of plagues that William Bramley explores in *The Gods of Eden*. The authors make no mention of extraterrestrial influence nor have any intention to discuss, prove or disprove the UFO pattern.

Tompkins, Peter.1976. *Mystery of the Mexican Pyramids*. Harper & Row Publishers, Inc., Perennial Library 10 East 53rd St. New York, NY 10022. ISBN: 0-06-091366-5 (Paperback), $18.95.
A treasure-trove of drawings, photos, history and speculation on the meaning of major finds from ancient Mexico. A fun and rich text which lends a unique interpretation of these past peoples' beliefs and practices.

Vallee, Jacques.1988. *Dimensions: A Casebook of Alien Contact*. Contemporary Books, Inc.,180 North Michigan Ave., Chicago, IL 60601. ISBN: 0-8092-4586-8 (hardcover).
The author, an astrophysicist, is a most highly respected UFO researcher. This book is a chronicle of encounter stories beginning in ancient history. Interesting Japanese encounters, not commonly described, shows again the similarities in contact past and present regardless of place.
———— 1991. *Revelations: Alien Contact and Human Deception*, Ballantine Books, Random House, 201 E. 50th St., New York, NY 10022. ISBN:0-345-37566-1 $4.99.

Walters, Ed & Francis. 1990. *The Gulf Breeze Sightings: The Most Amazing Sighting of UFOs in History*. William Morrow and Company Inc., 105 Madison Ave. New York, NY 10016. ISBN: 0-688-09087-7. $21.95.
The most scientifically photographed UFO images ever taken. With great dedication, the authors endured multiple frightening close encounters with UFOs. Ed discovered he had been abducted while pursuing this work. Great evidence.

Walton, Travis. 1978,1996. *Fire in the Sky*. Marlowe & Company, 632 Broadway, New York, NY 10012. ISBN: 1-56924-840-0. $24.95.
This updated version of Walton's abduction experience is riveting. The human drama that not only Travis experienced, but his friends and family experienced while he was missing. Includes seven corroborated polygraphs.

Acknowledgments

Any book requires a team of people committed to its publication. The team that contributed to this book required every human strength: courage, tolerance, open-mindedness, determination, integrity, and quest for truth. This team includes all UFO witnesses and the abductees, the artists and writers who have donated to the Museum, the publishers and authors in the bibliography, honest government officials... and military personnel, and those with quiet bravery we will never hear about.

This team also includes the extraterrestrial beings that apparently visit us. There is no question that humans, animals, and the earth have suffered trauma and death as a result of some of their visits; but, giving them the benefit of the doubt, let us persevere in our attempts to make distinctions between them and communicate with the benevolent ones through diplomacy—the same courtesies we try to extend to our allied-earth neighbors. We have so much to gain. Thanks especially to my translucent friend who touched me when I was eleven.

Thanks to my dear friends at the IUFOMRC who helped me compile, write and edit this information: Glenn Dennis, Walter Haut, Deon Crosby, Carol Syska, Miller Johnson, Dennis Balthaser, the Board of Directors, and all the volunteers at the IUFOMRC. Thank you also to the friendly merchants in the towns of Roswell and Portales, New Mexico. Special thanks to Colonel Philip Corso, who gave me his enthusiasm. Thanks also to Stanton Friedman for the detailed research information and corrections he so generously shared and Walter Andrus, Jr., who gave me his support on such short notice.

Without the witnesses, artists, writers, and contributors there would be no Museum. Thank you to the founding 100 members. (See list pages 150-151.) Heartfelt appreciation to all the artists and writers who allowed their work to be reprinted in this guide.

Deepest gratitude to all my family who provide me with roots for sustenance in my life, but especially: Gordon Leacock, Mike & Rick Perry, and Telzey; Marge & Bob Giebitz, Bob & Teresa Dilmore, Lydia, Spencer & Ben Schaeffer, Linda, John, Jennifer & Julie Tribbey, Robby, Tammy, Tess & Robby III Dilmore, Mark, Debbi & Sarah Dilmore & Thomas See, Allison & Joey Ellis & Alaina Tomberlin, Gordon & Sue Dilmore, Sheila, Dave, Mark & Lisa DeJohn, Bob, Jeanne, Nina, Niki & Lexi Leacock, Jean & John Whittier, John & Debby Renner, Marg, Heidi & Kaleb Dilmore, and Arian Horbovetz.

Friends are the family you choose. Thanks to each and every one of mine past and present for your support. I really appreciate those of you who have encouraged me while I've worked on this book: Jean & Dave Ballou, Marc Barasch, Cheryl Bow, (Barry) Michael Comer, Leigh Daniels & Evie Gauthier, Kay, Mike and Jason Duika, Karla Groesbeck, Jane Hill, Annie Hiniker, Fred & Ila Hornstra, John Kilar, Betz King, Jamie & David Kryscynski, Sue, John & Christina Lee, Arlene Malvitz, Vican & Mary Matossian, John & Jean Perry, Henry Reed, Matt Rosen, Liz Sayre-King, Jonathan Scott, Mary Seibert, Marj Smith, Mark Smith, Ruth Wiskind, Rosie, Dan, Meggie & Eamon Wright, David, Mary, Ryan & Kathryn Yamamoto, and Debora & Lisa.

Special thanks to all the professionals whose support I received: Sue Lee, Susan Davenport-Geer, Barb Gunia, Richard Vore, Charles Baltimore, Aaron Kiley, Jim Oehl, John Endahl, Ben Willmore, Kathy King, Jan Stevens, Jean Schroeder, Janet P. Smith, Susan Weyman, and Martha Edwards. You each have a unique gift to offer.

Remembrances of love to my grandparents, Hermon & Helen Dilmore Sr., Harry & Florence Bacon, my uncle Hermon Dilmore Jr., to my aunt Judy Bacon and to my father and mother-in-law, Dr. Robert & Kathleen Leacock.

100 Founding Members of the IUFOMRC

Jean & O. W. "Bill" Adams
Hugh J. & Shirley Barker
Martha and Dick Bean
Mr. & Mrs. C.J.
  Beauchemin
Mr. and Mrs. Cory Beck
Richard A. Benham
W. Charles Bennett
Don Berliner
Sharon & Rick Biskynis
Lana & Danny Boswell
Robert W. Brown
Brandon Buckner
Goldie Buckner
Norman & Toodie Burke
Annabel & Ralph
  Burnworth
Glenn Campbell
Karen & Jerry Castillo
Betty & Jim Claypool
Zack Clem
Everett Clement
Peter C. Crosson
Pat & Bill Deets
Kay & Glenn Dennis
Florine & Robert F.
  Dennis
Larry E. Dickey
Tom Dunlap
Cheri West Farmer
Mr. & Mrs. Spencer Fields
First Federal Savings
  Bank
Mr. & Mr. M. W. Ford
Stanton T. Friedman
Fund for UFO Research
Maxine & Larry Goodell
Sue Graham

Antonio Granados
Thomas N. E. Greville
William Grohowski
Martine Grost
Tom Hall, Jr.
Lawrence C. Harris
Sally & Jim Hartman
Walter & Lorraine R. Haut
Ray Helgesen
Mr. & Mrs. E.P. "Bud"
  Herring
Linda & John T. Hinkle
Thomas E. Jennings
Timothy Z. Jennings
Dr. & Mrs. Emmit
  Jennings
Miller C. & Marilyn
  Johnson
Durwood O. Jones
Kent Jeffrey
Mr. & Mrs. S.P.
  Johnson III
Steinar Karlsen, Bruce
  Meland
John H. & Betty M. King
Oscar R.P. Lara
Joan H. Laurino
Dr. Jo Ann Levitt
Mr. & Mrs. Del Lewis
Max Littel
Dr. Thomas Longwill
Dr. Bruce Maccabee
Dr. & Mrs. Steve Marshall
L.W. & Edith McGuffin
Nancy & Linton Miller
Maurine Mitchell
Dr. & Mrs. A.L. Mulliken
Sarah E. Murdock

Tad Nakanishi
Polly & Gary Owen
Betty & Tom Pearson
Toni & Mike Pemberton
Gretchen & Ron Phillips
Lucille Pipkin
Inga F. Pyle
Kevin Randle
Sheila & David Roe
Mr. & Mrs. John F. Russell II
Toni L. & Del K. Rykert
Don Schmitt
Jerry Seller
Jean Sider
Keith J. Sjosten
Alma Spence
Jane & Sam Spencer
P. David Spiek
Edna & Tom P. Stephens
E. Pearl Stoll
Mary L. & Lloyd E. Stone
Ella & H.D. Storms
W.C. Taylor
Sherlea & Paul Taylor
Sally & Penrod Toles
Elizabeth Tulk
George S. Vogen
Lewis West
J. Phelps White III
Mr. & Mrs. Philip L. White
Fred Whiting
Pickett & Frank Young

Index

Author's note

I researched the available literature for the facts in this book. If you find an error that you can clarify with documentation please contact me:

C.P. Leacock
c/o Novel Writing Publishers
622 W. Liberty St. Ste. 11
Ann Arbor, MI 48103-4347
email: nwp@novelwriting.com
fax# 734-761-8540.

I will endeavor to keep this guide up to date, factual, and accurate. Corrections will be made in future editions.

Checkout the webpage: www.novelwriting.com
